Things that Jesus said

Parables of the Kingdom and Eternal Life

Doug Rowston

Rowston, Doug
THINGS THAT JESUS SAID
Parables of the Kingdom & Eternal Life

Published by
Grace & Peace Books
4A Wurilba Ave Hawthorn SA 5062 Australia
djrowston@gmail.com

© Douglas James Rowston 2016

This work is copyright. Other than for the purposes and subject to the conditions prescribed under the Copyright Act, no part of it may in any form or by any means (electronic, mechanical, microcopying, photocopying, recording or otherwise) be reproduced, stored in a retrieval system or transmitted without prior written permission from the publisher.

First published 2016 by Morning Star Publishing
This edition published in 2022

ISBN 978-0-6453288-5-1

This book is dedicated to Laurie

What is it like to be a citizen of the Kingdom of God? What is likely to happen on a given day? How are citizens expected to behave? How is the Kingdom of God different from other realms on our planet—past or present? And where do we find this kingdom in the context of our present world of complex and competing kingdoms?

I suggest you read Doug Rowston's new book, *Things that Jesus said*. Rowston analyses the parables of Jesus in the first three Gospels focusing on the key kingdom symbol of each parable, the background of that symbol and how that symbol may be relevant even today. For example, the parable of the labourers in the vineyard is about 'the grace of God's kingdom' and 'reveals the good news of Jesus in a nutshell'. Other parables will reveal that forgiveness is a way of life in the kingdom or that the kingdom is something really valuable, a hidden treasure to be discovered.

In Part B of his book, Rowston explores parables in John's Gospel which he describes as parables of eternal life. Many scholars have not identified these passages as parables, but Rowston demonstrates the connection with the parables in the first three gospels. In sum: The Gospels of Matthew, Mark and Luke tell Jesus' parables about God's kingdom. John's Gospel tells parables of Jesus, 'who is the king of God's kingdom and brings God's kind of life' (p. 94).

For example, The Parable of the Night Breeze is embodied in the 'wind blowing where it chooses' (John 3.8) and describes the coming of the life of God's new age. Rowston interprets the image of a woman in labour and in childbirth (John 16.21) as a parable relating to the crisis of the life of God's new age. The interpretation of these passages from John—and eleven more—as embodying parables is a rich, original and refreshing reading of the colourful imagery in the words of Jesus in John.

Rowston's readings of the explicit and implicit parables of the Gospel is a profound and readable analysis, appropriate for both meditation and serious group study.

Dr. Norman Habel *Professorial Fellow Flinders University, Adelaide, South Australia*

An illuminating and distinctive introduction not only to the parables of Jesus in all four Gospels but to the gospel itself. Grounded in excellent scholarship and engagingly written, *Things that Jesus said* deserves wide usage in church and seeker study groups.

> **Dr. E. Glenn Hinson** *Professor Emeritus of Spirituality and John Loftis Professor of Church History Baptist Theological Seminary at Richmond, Virginia*

Doug Rowston has given us a "pearl of great price" – a brief but comprehensive book on the parables of Jesus filled with not so hidden treasures: the texts of the various forms of the parables for easy reference, a brief exposition of each parable, fresh insights into their message and relevance today, a prayer related to each one, and questions for discussion. Best of all he does not neglect the parables in the Gospel of John, as have most other books on the parables. It is an ideal book for Bible study groups.

> **Dr. R. Alan Culpepper** *Dean Emeritus and Professor Emeritus of New Testament McAfee School of Theology, Mercer University, Atlanta, Georgia*

As an introduction to Jesus' parables, the book *Things that Jesus said* is both scholarly and practical. It is also quite clear that the author, Dr. Doug Rowston, writes from a background of being a serious student/scholar ... and a competent and enthusiastic preacher, teacher and lecturer. (He tells us that he also enjoys sharing the stories of the parables with his grandchildren!) As well as some excellent quotations from great scholars, the book contains many relevant anecdotes and reflections. To quote the American writer Frederick Buechner, "a parable is a small story with a large point." Doug Rowston takes those small stories, and helps his readers discover and explore the large point Jesus was making.

> **Rev. Barrie Hibbert** *Former Pastor of Flinders Street Baptist Church, Adelaide and Bloomsbury Central Baptist Church, London*

The parables of Jesus we receive through the gospel traditions have an enduring enigmatic quality that defy simple explanations. They provoke many questions and reflections on the part of the hearer, while providing windows into the kingdom of God. An understanding of the range of parabolic forms, together with significant background information deepens our engagement with the teachings of Jesus. Doug Rowston has provided a very accessible and well-informed "tour guide" to the parables of Jesus, striking a helpful balance in which commentary does not obscure the richness of the parables themselves. Highly recommended!

> **Bishop Tim Harris** *Research Fellow, St Barnabas College, Adelaide, South Australia*

In *Things that Jesus said: Parables of the Kingdom and Eternal Life* Doug Rowston takes his readers on a serious and challenging look at the gamut of stories that Jesus told as recorded in the New Testament. He is meticulous in his facilitation of our understanding of what these parables meant in Jesus's own setting, and for how the early church used them. He ranges from the Synoptic versions of the story of the Sower to the Johannine story of the woman in childbirth.

From that foundation Doug challenges his readers to make the connection to themselves as followers of that same Jesus but within the complexities of modern life. Each story ends with a corporate prayer and a short series of questions well worth individual reflection but even better for group discussion.

This volume is a worthy successor to earlier publications such as *Pray and Sing: Prayers and Songs in the New Testament* and *Promises and Blessings in the Book of Revelation*. It will be a helpful source for those interested in their own growth of understanding commitment to following Jesus. It is also a tool for helping others to grow.

> **Dr. Rosalind Gooden** *Former ABMS Missionary in Pakistan/ Bangladesh and former Director of Personnel and Training at Moore Potter House.*

Acknowledgements

The front cover image *Head of Christ* was painted by Rembrandt van Rijn in 1648.

The ink sketches of the sower and the shepherd were drawn by Craig Bowyer during the author's time as teacher at Prince Alfred College in Adelaide. They are reproduced with his permission.

Bible quotations are from The New Revised Standard Version Bible, copyright 1989, 1995 by the Division of Christian Education of the National Council of Churches of Christ in the U S A. Used by permission. All rights reserved.

CONTENTS

Introduction	11
Part A: Synoptic Parables	13
Parables of the Kingdom in the Gospels according to Matthew, Mark and Luke	14
1 The Sower	18
2 The Mustard Seed	27
3 The Hidden Treasure and the Costly Pearl	32
4 The Unforgiving Servant	37
5 The Labourers in the Vineyard	43
6 The Talents and the Pounds	49
7 The Sheep and the Goats	56
8 The Seed Growing Secretly	62
9 The Good Samaritan	68
10 The Rich Fool	75
11 The Prodigal Son	81
12 The Rich Man and Lazarus	89
13 The Pharisee and the Tax Collector	95

Part B: Johannine Parables	101
Parables of Eternal Life in the Gospel according to John	102
1 The Night Breeze	105
2 The Bridegroom and the Best Man	110
3 The Ripe Fields	115
4 The Apprentice Son	121
5 The Slave and the Son	127
6 The Shepherd and the Stranger	132
7 The Traveller in the Dark	138
8 The Grain of Wheat	143
9 The Walker at Sunset	148
10 The Bathtub and the Basin	153
11 The Father's House	158
12 The True Vine	163
13 The Woman in Childbirth	168
Conclusion	173
Select Bibliography	175

INTRODUCTION

Things that Jesus said is written against the background of a lifetime's interest in the stories of Jesus. At Sunday School and in church services I learnt what Jesus did and said according to the Gospels of Matthew, Mark, Luke and John. I could identify with the words of Paul, When I was a child, I spoke like a child, I thought like a child, I reasoned like a child (1 Corinthians 13:11a). I basically heard and read the Gospels without analysing the content. At theological college and then in doctoral studies, things changed, as I asked questions and found answers by utilising the tools of biblical research. In other words, in the words of Paul, when I became an adult, I put an end to childish ways (1 Corinthians 13:11b). All of this was the usual stage of human development which goes from concrete to abstract thinking.

Now while I read the stories of Jesus with grandchildren, I realise that they are in the stage of thinking concretely of the content of these stories. In time they will move to the process of thinking abstractly about the meaning of the stories. Obviously, this book about the parables of Jesus is not written for children. If one requires Bible stories written for young children, I recommend the likes of The Lost Sheep Series written by my friend Andrew McDonough. My grandchildren love his version of the parable of the good Samaritan! However, in this book for adults, we ask questions and find answers about parables of Jesus.

The parables of Jesus include figurative sayings, similitudes, and story-parables. *Things that Jesus said* treats parables of Jesus in all four Gospels. Usually, most scholars think of parables restricted to the first three Gospels, the Synoptic Gospels. The first half of this book examines Synoptic parables about the coming and growth, grace and mercy, citizens and crisis of the kingdom of God. Unusually, a few scholars identify parables in the Fourth Gospel. This book is in the unusual category. In the second half there is an analysis of Johannine parables about the coming, enduring love, sharers and crisis of the life of the age that comes in Jesus.

Things that Jesus said is indebted to my experience as a theological lecturer at Burleigh College, a religious education teacher at Prince Alfred College, a pastor at Richmond Baptist Church, and an adjunct lecturer at St Barnabas College (Charles Sturt University). I have found inspiration for my approach from, among others, C.H. Dodd, Joachim Jeremias, A.M. Hunter, Peter Rhea Jones, Arland Hultgren, William Hull, Alan Culpepper, and Ben Witherington. I thank my wife Rosalie for her patience and love during the writing of this book. I am also extremely grateful to my brother Laurie for his meticulous checking of the completed draft of this work. I trust that my readers come to appreciate the Synoptic and Johannine parables as provocative, dynamic and creative.

Doug Rowston

PART A: SYNOPTIC PARABLES

The Sower

PARABLES OF THE KINGDOM IN THE GOSPELS ACCORDING TO MATTHEW, MARK AND LUKE

Jesus is known as a master storyteller. He tells parables which compare everyday events with events of eternal importance. Some parables are short pithy proverbs about the blind leading the blind, specks and logs, trees and fruit, building houses on rock and sand, and so on. Other parables are long catchy stories. He says that God's kingdom is like events in the life of a farmer or a landlord or a king or a landowner or a traveller or a family or a wealthy person or worship at the temple. His parables are stories from real life: farmers sow crops, landlords lease properties, kings settle accounts, landowners hire labourers, travellers go down dangerous roads, families have children who stray or stay, wealthy people are selfish or generous, worshippers are proud or humble.

His parables challenge his hearers to stop and think about what they are doing with their lives. Are they committing themselves to the cause of Jesus permanently? Do they find God's kingdom by accident or by searching? Are they putting God's gifts to use? Are they doing something also for unimportant people? Do they care for their needy neighbour regardless of race and nationality? Do they personally appear to be near to God but are actually far from him? Are they piling up riches for themselves while not being rich towards God? Are they making themselves important and not being humble?

His parables focus on a main idea, in figures of speech or comparisons or stories. They comment on the meaning of God's rule in the time and place of Jesus. They are repeated as his witnesses apply the message about Jesus to their time and place in the Roman Empire. The parables tell of the rule of God which comes and grows in the work of Jesus, the grace and mercy of God which extends to all through Jesus, the kind of citizens who live under the rule of God, and the hour of decision in view of the judgement and victory of God starting to be realised in Jesus.

To follow Jesus is to identify with the coming and growth of God's kingdom. In Jesus' life and teaching the kingdom of God is being inaugurated but not yet completed. To follow Jesus is to experience the grace and mercy of God. Jesus seeks and saves the lost. Those who repent are forgiven. Those who are saved trust and obey Jesus. To follow Jesus is to be a citizen under the rule of God. Such citizens are fully committed to Jesus; they serve him obediently, they trust him victoriously. Those who follow Jesus also decide for him in the crises of life and death where decisions are ultimate and of eternal consequence.

The parables convey the authentic teaching of Jesus in masterly fashion and have perennial relevance. We still talk about the talents, the sheep and the goats, the good Samaritan, the prodigal son. The parables of Jesus are unforgettable, whether they are short or long. They still cause us to think and to act on their message.

It is worth noting that the parables are not allegories, but they may contain allegorical features. They usually have a major idea. However, there may be accompanying parallels. Today we do not read the parable of the good Samaritan as Augustine did 1600 years ago. He interpreted ordinary details in the earthly story as symbolic truths for people with spiritual knowledge.

> *A man* [Adam] *was going down from Jerusalem* [the heavenly city of peace] *to Jericho* [the moon], *and fell into the hands of robbers* [the devil and his angels], *who stripped him* [of his immortality], *beat him* [persuaded him to sin], *and went away, leaving him half dead* [knowing God but being oppressed by sin] . *Now by chance a priest* [Old Testament priesthood] *was going down that road; and when he saw him, he passed by on the other side. So likewise a Levite* [Old Testament ministry], *when he came to the place and saw him, passed by on the other side. But a Samaritan* [meaning Guardian, the Lord himself] *while travelling came near him; and when he saw him, he was moved with pity. He went to him and bandaged his wounds* [restraining sin], *having poured oil* [comfort of hope] *and wine* [exhortation to work] *on them. Then he put him on his own animal* [belief in the incarnation], *brought him to an inn* [the church], *and took care of him. The next day* [after the resurrection] *he took out two denarii* [either love for God and neighbour or this life and the next], *gave them to the innkeeper* [Paul the Apostle}, *and said, 'Take care of him; and when I come back, I will repay you whatever more you spend* [either celibacy or manual work] .

Nobody interprets the good Samaritan like that now! Today, we would note the major idea of being a good neighbour and the accompanying parallels to priest, Levite and Samaritan in our time and place. So, it is necessary to repeat that the parables are not allegories, but they may contain allegorical features. They usually have a major idea. However, they may have accompanying parallels to enhance the story, to include listeners or readers in the story. The parables of Jesus are told for our learning so that we might hear, read, mark, learn and inwardly digest their message of God's kingdom, by grace, through faith, in hope, with love.

As we consider parables told in the Synoptic Gospels, we shall draw upon the insights of C.H. Dodd, Joachim Jeremias, Helmut Thielicke, A.M. Hunter, Kenneth Bailey, Robert Farrar Capon, Craig Blomberg, Peter Rhea Jones, Arland Hultgren, and Klyne Snodgrass. We shall find that the parables do not hide their meaning but they are not just illustrations. They are provocative, dynamic and creative. The parables involve the hearer and the reader with a view to commitment.

1   THE SOWER

Listen! A sower went out to sow. And as he sowed, some seeds fell on the path, and the birds came and ate them up. Other seeds fell on rocky ground, where they did not have much soil, and they sprang up quickly, since they had no depth of soil. But when the sun rose, they were scorched; and since they had no root, they withered away. Other seeds fell among thorns, and the thorns grew up and choked them. Other seeds fell on good soil and brought forth grain, some a hundredfold, some sixty, some thirty. Hear then the parable of the sower. When anyone hears the word of the kingdom and does not understand it, the evil one comes and snatches away what is sown in the heart; this is what was sown on the path. As for what was sown on rocky ground, this is the one who hears the word and immediately receives it with joy; yet such a person has no root, but endures only for a while, and when trouble or persecution arises on account of the word, that person immediately falls away. As for what was sown among thorns, this is the one who hears the word, but the cares of the world and the lure of wealth choke the word, and it yields nothing. But as for what was sown on good soil, this is the one who hears the word and understands it, who indeed bears fruit and yields, in one case a hundredfold, in another sixty, and in another thirty.
Matthew 13:3-8, 18-23

Listen! A sower went out to sow. And as he sowed, some seed fell on the path, and the birds came and ate it up. Other seed fell on rocky ground, where it did not have much soil, and it sprang up quickly, since it had no depth of soil. And when the sun rose, it was scorched; and since it had no root, it withered away. Other seed fell among thorns, and the thorns grew up and choked it, and it yielded no grain. Other seed fell into good soil and brought forth grain, growing up and increasing and yielding thirty and sixty and a hundredfold. Do you not understand this parable? Then how will you understand all the parables? The sower sows the word. These are the ones on the path where the word is sown: when they hear, Satan immediately comes and takes away the word that is sown in them. And these are the ones sown on rocky ground: when they hear the word, they immediately receive it with joy. But they have no root, and endure only for a while; then, when trouble or persecution arises on account of the word, immediately they fall away. And others are those sown among the thorns: these are the ones who hear the word, but the cares of the world, and the lure of wealth, and the desire for other things come in and choke the word, and it yields nothing. And these are the ones sown on the good soil: they hear the word and accept it and bear fruit, thirty and sixty and a hundredfold.
Mark 4:3-8, 13-20

A sower went out to sow his seed; and as he sowed, some fell on the path and was trampled on, and the birds of the air ate it up. Some fell on the rock; and as it grew up, it withered for lack of moisture. Some fell among thorns, and the thorns grew with it and choked it. Some fell into good soil, and when it grew, it produced a hundredfold. Now the parable is this: The seed is the word of God. The ones on the path are those who have heard; then the devil comes and takes away the word from their hearts, so that they may not believe and be saved. The ones on the rock are those who, when they hear the word, receive it with joy. But these have no root; they believe only for a while and in a time of testing fall away. As for what fell among the thorns, these are the ones who hear; but as they go on their way, they are choked by the cares and riches and pleasures of life, and their fruit does not mature. But as for that in the good soil, these are the ones who, when they hear the word, hold it fast in an honest and good heart, and bear fruit with patient endurance.
Luke 8:5-8, 11-15

Category: What type of parable is it?

The majority of modern scholars have tended to distinguish between the parable and the interpretation given in the gospels. They see only the parable, not the attached interpretation, as the product of Jesus himself. Accordingly, the parable of the sower tells the story of a farmer's fortunes. It is a parable of growth. By contrasting the start and finish of the agricultural season it assures the farmer of an abundant harvest and challenges the soils to be productive. It is a parable about the coming and the growth of the kingdom, a story to encourage the proclaimers of the kingdom.

The minority of modern scholars accept that both the parable of the sower and its interpretation go back to Jesus in some form. This parable provides an impetus to hearing and hoping. It is about the certain coming of the kingdom. Although the interpretation is applied anew by the early church, it is quite possible that the parable's explanation originates with Jesus. It is a collection of four images which provoke thought and action. The parable of the sower and its interpretation may be entitled 'Sower, Seed, Soils, Spin-off.' It is about the coming of God's kingdom in the person of the King's Son. As we shall see, it makes its listeners and readers think about their response to the rule of God.

Context: When and where is the parable's situation?

There are two main life situations of the parable of the sower. First is its setting in the life and ministry of Jesus. The ministry of Jesus includes his words and deeds taking place in Galilee and Judea and culminating in Jerusalem. Second is its setting in the life and mission of the church. Part of the mission of the church includes the editing of the Gospels for the purpose of telling converted and unconverted, friends and foes about Jesus.

The scholars who separate the parable from its interpretation propose a move from Jesus to the church. The parable thus speaks in particulars with its encouragement of an excellent harvest and the interpretation speaks in general terms with its warning of testing conditions. The parable tells of a triumphant end in face of repeated failure and the interpretation speaks of four classes of response. Modern scholars maximise the parable and minimise the interpretation. The setting of the parable is the ups and downs of the Galilean ministry with possibly a dual message: have faith in God and take heed how you hear. The parable encourages proclamation while the interpretation raises the issue of reception.

The scholars who are prepared to see Jesus' mind and thought behind both the parable and the interpretation propose continuity rather than discontinuity. The interpretation fits the parable. Jesus creates the story and its explanation. The Gospel writers shape the inclusion of both. According to the Gospels, Jesus tells the parable to *great crowds* (Matthew 13:2), to *a very large crowd* (Mark 4:1), and to *a great crowd* (Luke 8:4). Jesus interprets the parable to *the disciples* (Matthew 13:10), *those who were around him along with the twelve* (Mark 4:10), and *his disciples* (Luke 8:9).

In summary, the life situation of the parable of the sower and its interpretation focusses the reader's attention on the ministry of Jesus with its success in the midst of failure and response to the teaching of Jesus and on the mission of the early church with its own witness in the midst of struggle and response.

Content: How is the parable to be understood?

The parable of the sower with its interpretation appears in the first three Gospels. Mark 4 is probably the earliest version and emphasises the farmer sowing *seed*, which is *the word*. Matthew 13 utilises Mark 4, abbreviates the parable and expands the interpretation to emphasise the different responses to *the word of the kingdom* by its mention of bad and good *soil*. Luke 8 also shortens Mark 4 and, in the process, equates *the seed* with *the word of God*.

In the time of Jesus the farmer would carry his seed in a bag over his shoulder or under his arm and broadcast it by hand as he walked across his small plot of land. The seed would fall on the path, on the rocky ground, among thorns and in good soil. According to Joachim Jeremias, the farmer would then plough the seed on the path, on the rocky ground, among thorns and in good soil. In other words, sowing preceded ploughing. Although this method was wasteful, at the end of the season the good soil produced an abundant harvest. The hearers of the parable of Jesus would identify with the agricultural customs of the time.

Between the parable and its interpretation Matthew, Mark and Luke include a quotation from the Old Testament to give the reason for speaking in parables. *Keep listening, but do not comprehend; keep looking, but do not understand. Make the mind of this people dull, and stop their ears, and shut their eyes, so that they may not look with their eyes, and listen with their ears, and comprehend with their minds, and turn and be healed. (Isaiah 6:9-10)* Isaiah was referring to the inevitable, not the intended, result of his message in the eighth century BC. The quotation in the Gospels has the same purpose. It does not mean the intended result of the parables of Jesus, but, in fact, it does mean their inevitable result. Jesus gives his listeners the choice between truly listening by mulling over the meaning of parables, or turning a deaf ear by ignoring the intention of parables. The former choose to use it and the latter choose to lose it. By way of explanation, 'it' refers to being open to God's future possibilities through faith in Jesus. Each Gospel gives an interpretation of the parable. With a little imagination it is possible to picture the following scenario.[1] As the original hearers contemplated the meaning of the parable, they would have known the words of the ancient confession of faith: Hear, O Israel: The LORD is our God, the LORD alone.

---

[1] See C.F.D. Moule, 'Mark 4:1-20 Yet Once More .' *Neotestamentica et Semitica* (T . & T . Clark, 1969), pp . 95-113, for the comparison of the parable's interpretation with Deuteronomy 6:5-6 .

You shall love the LORD your God with all your heart, and with all your soul, and with all your might. (Deuteronomy 6:5-6)

Following Matthew's version, we read about the unsuccessful sowing of *the word of the kingdom*. First, some hear but don't understand. *The evil one comes and snatches away what is sown in the heart; this is what was sown on the path.* They have not heard with all their heart. Second, others hear joyfully but the joy only lasts for a short time. *As for what was sown on rocky ground, when trouble or persecution arises on account of the word, that person immediately falls away.* They have not heard with all their soul. Third, others hear but are distracted. *As for what was sown among thorns, this is the one who hears the word, but the cares of the world and the lure of wealth choke the word, and it yields nothing.* They have not heard with all their might.

However, we also read in Matthew's version about the successful sowing of *the word of the kingdom*. There are those who hear, do understand, and are fruitful in word and deed. *As for what was sown on good soil, this is the one who hears the word and understands it, who indeed bears fruit and yields, in one case a hundredfold, in another sixty, and in another thirty.* They have heard with all their heart, and with all their soul, and with all their might. After their initial response such people of faith have continued to live productively in word and deed.

There is another imaginative possibility. Klyne Snodgrass picks up the work of N.T. Wright who envisions the parable and its interpretation in the bigger picture of the Babylonian exile and the return from exile. There is a move from God sowing the seed through Jesus to God sowing people in Israel through a return from not physical but spiritual exile. According to N.T. Wright, there is a grand narrative about the kingdom of God which highlights this return from exile. It is a question of whether there are themes other than return from exile to explain the work and words of Jesus. There appear to be such themes in the ideas of mighty works, powerful words, sufferings, defeat of evil, final judgement and conquest of death. However, this is a matter of scholarly debate which is way beyond the scope of this small book.

Connection: Why does the parable apply now as it did then?

As we have thought about the category, the context and the content of the parable, we may now reflect upon its connection to our place and time. Applying the parable provides indications of its provocative, dynamic and creative nature. As readers, we respond to the parable out of its world setting into our world setting.

First, why does the sower trigger our imagination? Do we think of the earthly farmer as a picture of the Heavenly Father? The use of an agricultural figure of a farmer who sows seed is paralleled by the utilisation of a viticultural figure of a vinegrower who prunes grapevines in the Fourth Gospel. Jesus says, *I am the true vine, and my Father is the vinegrower. He removes every branch in me that bears no fruit. Every branch that bears fruit he prunes to make it bear more fruit. (John 15:1-2)* One thinks of the Jewish prayers to God as the creator of the grains from which bread is made and of the grapes from which wine is prepared: 'Blessed are you, LORD our God,

King of the universe, who brings forth bread from the earth' and 'Blessed are you, LORD our God, King of the universe, who creates the fruit of the vine.'

Second, why is the seed significant? Do we make the jump from the sowing of seed to the spreading of the Divine Word? In Luke's version of the parable's interpretation, *The seed is the word of God.* One is reminded of the words of Isaiah of Babylon: *For as the rain and the snow come down from heaven, and do not return there until they have watered the earth, making it bring forth and sprout, giving seed to the sower and bread to the eater, so shall my word be that goes out from my mouth; it shall not return to me empty, but it shall accomplish that which I purpose, and succeed in the thing for which I sent it. (Isaiah 55:10-11)*

Third, why are the soils diverse? Do we equate the bad and good soils with the negative and positive human responses? Desertion of the bad soil due to devilish misunderstanding, troubling persecution and worldly diversions is contrasted with perseverance of the good soil. It is possible that every one of us has in us all four types of soil. At different times of life we may well be hard or rocky or thorny or good soil. The lesson is: don't let the seed fall on the path, don't be shallow rocky ground, get rid of the thorns, be good soil! Respond to God's word with all that is within you!

Fourth, why is the spin-off variable? Do we contemplate the parallel of agricultural harvest and personal fruitfulness? Lasting reception of the seed leads to an increasing harvest, to the bearing of much fruit. Whether we read the yield of the harvest as *some a hundredfold, some sixty, some thirty*

(Matthew), or *thirty and sixty and a hundredfold* (Mark), or *a hundredfold* (Luke), the point is the contrast between what is sown and what is grown. The parable is a word of encouragement to the people who are unduly pessimistic: God's message will triumph, God's messenger is crucified but does rise from the dead. The parable is also a challenge to people who are simplistically optimistic. God's message requires receptivity and fruitfulness. It must be heard, held fast *in an honest and good heart*, and bear fruit *with patient endurance*.

Prayer

Our Creating and Redeeming God, we thank you for reminding us that you are interested in us all as we face the mysteries of life, that you are at work in our world, that you encourage us to let you into our lives, and that you challenge us to be fruitful followers of Jesus, your Son, our Lord and Saviour. Help us to have faith in you and to take heed how we hear your message. Amen.

Discussion

1. How does the parable of the sower add to our understanding of the kingdom of God?
2. Why did Jesus originally tell the parable of the sower?
3. What does the parable of the sower say to us in our world?

2 THE MUSTARD SEED

The kingdom of heaven is like a mustard seed that someone took and sowed in his field; it is the smallest of all the seeds, but when it has grown it is the greatest of shrubs and becomes a tree, so that the birds of the air come and make nests in its branches.
Matthew 13:31-32

With what can we compare the kingdom of God, or what parable will we use for it? It is like a mustard seed, which, when sown upon the ground, is the smallest of all the seeds on earth; yet when it is sown it grows up and becomes the greatest of all shrubs, and puts forth large branches, so that the birds of the air can make nests in its shade.
Mark 4:30-32

What is the kingdom of God like? And to what should I compare it? It is like a mustard seed that someone took and sowed in the garden; it grew and became a tree, and the birds of the air made nests in its branches.
Luke 13:18-19

Category: What type of parable is it?

The parable is about the coming and growth of the kingdom of God. It provides great assurance to the hearers of the parable by contrasting the tiny mustard seed with the mature shrub or large tree. The insignificant present kingdom will grow into the formidable future kingdom. However, the parable does not talk about progress or development over the years. It does contrast something very small at the beginning with something very big at the end.

Context: When and where is the parable's situation?

Mark's version in the present tense can be explained in terms of the time of Jesus. Jesus is giving an analogy. The mustard seed is sown, it grows, it becomes a shrub. The primary life situation of the parable of the mustard seed is in the life and ministry of Jesus. How can the small band of the followers of Jesus find encouragement in that God's new age is coming?

The version of Matthew and Luke is in the past tense. The mustard seed was sown, it grew, it became a tree. The early church is retelling the parable. The secondary life situation of the parable of the mustard seed is in the mission and witness of the early church. How can the small groups of Christians be sure that their cause will survive against the might of the Roman Empire?

The reader will note that Matthew refers to *the kingdom of heaven* rather than *the kingdom of God*. The probable reason is that the evangelist avoids using the name of God according to Jewish reverential practice lest the divine name be used dishonourably. There is no other difference between the phrases *kingdom of heaven* and *kingdom of God*.

Content: How is the parable to be understood?

The inconspicuous, a mustard seed, the kingdom in the present, contrasts with the conspicuous, the mustard bush, the kingdom in the future. On the one hand, the mustard seed is called *the smallest of all the seeds*. It is a midget among seeds. Between 725 and 760 mustard seeds weigh one gram. There are smaller seeds, but Jesus is speaking proverbially, not literally. On the other hand, the mustard bush is called *the greatest of all shrubs*. Indeed, it becomes *a tree* (Matthew and Luke) with *branches* (Matthew, Mark and Luke). It is huge among herbs. The mustard bush grows to a height of 2.5 to 3 metres.

The original hearers would know a high tree as a symbol of a great empire in the Old Testament: *All the birds of the air made their nests in its boughs; under its branches all the animals of the field gave birth to their young; and in its shade all great nations lived. (Ezekiel 31:6) Its foliage was beautiful, its fruit abundant, and it provided food for all. The animals of the field found shade under it, the birds of the air nested in its branches, and from it all living beings were fed. (Daniel 4:12)* Jesus applies the symbol of a large mustard plant to the blessings of the rule of God which are available to all, both Jew and Gentile: *the birds of the air come and make nests in its branches.*

Jesus is appealing to the imagination of his hearers. He contrasts what is inconspicuous, a mustard seed, and what will be conspicuous, the mustard bush. The disciples would remember the comment of Jesus about associating with 'bad characters' within Israel: *Those who are well have no need of a physician, but those who are sick; I have come to call not the righteous but sinners. (Mark 2:17)* The disciples of Jesus would also think of his words about the inclusion of Gentiles beyond Israel: *I tell you, many will come from east and west and will eat with Abraham and Isaac and Jacob in the kingdom of heaven. (Matthew 8:11)*

Connection: Why does the parable apply now as it did then?

First, what is like a mustard seed? It is possible to point to tiny beginnings. Helmut Thielicke recalled his first Bible group as a young pastor in a Lutheran Church during the Nazi regime in Germany. He was faced with two very old ladies and an even older church organist. Was this a valid indication of the all powerful Christ to whom all authority had been given in heaven and on earth? It was a far cry from the great theologian and gifted preacher that he became.

In telling the story of Martha Berry and Henry Ford, Peter Rhea Jones speaks of "the infinitude of the little" and "the legacy of possibility". Martha asked the carmaker for a million dollars to help the poor in the mountains of Georgia. Ford gave her ten cents. She bought a bag of peanuts and planted them. Next year the whole crop of peanuts was planted in a bigger field. Eventually she packed the peanuts and sold them at a roadside market. Then she wrote another letter to Ford in which she said: 'Remember the ten cents? Well, sir, I invested the money in peanuts, and we made enough to buy a piano for our music students. Isn't that a good dividend?' Ford was so impressed that he made the donation of one million dollars.

Second, what is like a bush for birds? It is possible to see big outcomes. Helmut Thielicke thought of a palm tree in the Tübingen botanical gardens. The palm outgrew its glasshouse. Another storey of glass had to be added. Sooner or later yet another layer of glass would be needed. An interesting contrast is the tale of the gum tree at Burnside shopping centre in suburban Adelaide. The gum was unable to survive the confines of its glass roof within the shopping mall. Attempts to provide the tree with fresh air and adequate water failed dismally. The giant gum tree died and had to be removed. The Tübingen palm and the Burnside gum both required air and water with sufficient room to grow. Both needed to follow the example of the tiny mustard seed which grew into the giant mustard plant.

The kingdom of God is not to be confined to pious circles but is to be let loose in the world of men, women and children inside and outside the church. Christianity then is a striking example of small beginnings and great endings. The church can be an agent of the kingdom. The followers of Jesus have spread to the ends of the earth. The kingdom has thus made its presence real in world history.

Prayer

Our Creating and Redeeming God, we thank you for the mustard seed sown in the field, sown in a hidden way, growing up into the mustard bush for birds, resulting in individual and communal transformation despite hostile opposition. Let loose your kingdom in the world of men and women, boys and girls. May your rule not just survive, may it thrive inside and outside the church. We pray in the name of Jesus. Amen.

Discussion

1. How does the parable of the mustard seed contribute to our insights into the kingdom of God?
2. Why did Jesus originally tell the parable of the mustard seed?
3. What is the relevance of the parable of the mustard seed today?

3   THE HIDDEN TREASURE AND THE COSTLY PEARL

The kingdom of heaven is like treasure hidden in a field, which someone found and hid; then in his joy he goes and sells all that he has and buys that field. Again, the kingdom of heaven is like a merchant in search of fine pearls; on finding one pearl of great value, he went and sold all that he had and bought it.
Matthew 13:44-46

Category: What type of parables are they?

The parables are a couplet about finding the kingdom. They liken God's rule to a treasure hidden in a field and a very valuable pearl. They revolve around two diverse characters: one a poor day labourer and the other a rich dealer in pearls. Each gives up everything to acquire priceless worth. The word pictures convey the sort of people who truly belong to the reign of God. The twin parables are about the citizens of God's kingdom.

Context: When and where is the parables' situation?

On the one hand, Jesus is speaking in readily understandable terms about the kind of person who belongs in the kingdom. The Roman provinces of Galilee and Judea were subject to wartime conditions before and after the life of Jesus. In such conditions it was a commonsense precaution to bury treasure in the ground or to hide it in caves. The Jewish historian, Josephus, records the finding of treasures stored beneath the ground by the Roman occupiers and conquerors in the first century. Furthermore, Galilee and Judea were on the trade routes for buyers and sellers. Pearls from the Red Sea, the

Persian Gulf and the Indian Ocean were highly valued. The first century writer, Pliny the Elder, mentions pearls as the most valuable goods and, in the second century, Arrianus says that pearls are worth three times as much as gold.

On the other hand, Matthew's Gospel retells the twin parables in a format that is inoffensive to first century Jewish readers. Whereas Mark and Luke refer to *the kingdom of God* in their versions of parables of the kingdom, Matthew refers to *the kingdom of heaven*. Jews to this day are hesitant to use the divine name. I have seen a sign in English on the Temple Mount in Jerusalem which read 'G-D' for 'GOD'. Accordingly, Matthew's Gospel generally prefers the words *the kingdom of heaven* out of respect for Jewish pious custom. There are only a few references to *the kingdom of God* in Matthew's Gospel.

Content: How are the parables to be understood?

The first parable is told in the present tense. A poor day labourer ploughs a field and his ox sinks into a hole. In the hole he finds a jar of silver jewels and coins. The jar has been hidden in the face of an invading army. The accidental finder joyfully puts the jar back underground and goes off to sell all his belongings for the sake of buying the plot of land. The treasure safely remains part of the field and is acquired by the day labourer on his purchase of the field.

The second parable is told in the past tense. A rich dealer in pearls searched long and hard for more of the same and found an especially valuable pearl. The deliberate finder counted the cost and sold everything he had with a single minded view to purchasing the pearl. The merchant on his return was satisfied to complete the transaction. His joy at finding the pearl may be implicit but his sacrifice of everything to buy the pearl is explicit.

Both parables seem to identify the kingdom of God with something really valuable. The joy of discovering the kingdom is obvious in the parable of the hidden treasure and may be assumed in the parable of the costly pearl. The kingdom is stumbled upon in the first and is searched for in the second. In both parables the finders decide that the kingdom is worth sacrificing everything to gain it. The original hearers are left to ask themselves a leading question: are they prepared to take the risk of giving up all for the sake of God's cause? The challenge is clear: *strive first for the kingdom of God and his righteousness, and all these things will be given to you as well. (Matthew 6:33)*

Connection: Why do the parables apply now as they did then?

Are we like people who stumble upon the treasure of the kingdom unawares? For some the message of Jesus comes, so to speak, out of a clear blue sky. Or, are we like people who search for the mysterious meaning of life deliberately and earnestly? For many the message of Jesus comes at the end of a long and winding road.

In 1952 the Copper Scroll was discovered in a cave two kilometres north of Qumran near the Dead Sea. It is a list of buried treasure written in Hebrew on three copper sheets riveted together as one and it was oxidised and could not be unrolled. It was finally opened for reading in 1956. Each of its

64 sections describes a treasure, such as gold and silver, and gives its hidden location. The Copper Scroll may well refer to the Jerusalem Temple's treasures hidden before the destruction of the Temple by the Romans in AD 70. Although none of these treasures has been found, the parable of the hidden treasure tells us of the finding of an everlasting treasure, the kingdom of God.

When the kingdom is found accidentally or deliberately, the finder realises its great value. There are questions to be answered. Are we willing to consider all else as secondary to the primary value of God's domain? Are we willing to commit ourselves sacrificially to the life and work of God's reign as followers of the teller of the parables?

Klyne Snodgrass tells the story of Roy Whetstine's experience . Roy collected precious stones. In 1986 his young sons gave him five dollars each to buy one for them at a Tucson, Arizona gem fair. He found a potato sized stone in a fifteen dollar bin. His offer of ten dollars was accepted. At first, Whetstine claimed that the stone was a 1905 carat star sapphire worth more than two million dollars. According to Snopes . com, the story was partly true. The stone has been cut, polished and named the Life and Pride of America's Star. It was probably worth a thousand dollars more or less . Whetstine's story makes us think of the parables of the hidden treasure and the costly pearl.

Prayer

Our Creating and Redeeming God, we thank you for the hidden treasure and the costly pearl of your kingdom. Some of us find it accidentally, others find it deliberately. Help us to consider all else as secondary to your domain and to commit ourselves sacrificially to your reign as followers of Jesus. May we seek first the kingdom of God and his righteousness. We pray in the name of Jesus. Amen.

Discussion

1. How do the parables of the hidden treasure and the costly pearl deepen our perceptions about the kingdom of God?
2. Why did Jesus originally tell the parables of the hidden treasure and the costly pearl?
3. What are contemporary meanings for us of the parables of the hidden treasure and the costly pearl?

4 THE UNFORGIVING SERVANT

For this reason the kingdom of heaven may be compared to a king who wished to settle accounts with his slaves. When he began the reckoning, one who owed him ten thousand talents was brought to him; and, as he could not pay, his lord ordered him to be sold, together with his wife and children and all his possessions, and payment to be made. So the slave fell on his knees before him, saying, 'Have patience with me, and I will pay you everything.' And out of pity for him, the lord of that slave released him and forgave him the debt. But that same slave, as he went out, came upon one of his fellow slaves who owed him a hundred denarii; and seizing him by the throat, he said, 'Pay what you owe.' Then his fellow slave fell down and pleaded with him, 'Have patience with me, and I will pay you.' But he refused; then he went and threw him into prison until he would pay the debt. When his fellow slaves saw what had happened, they were greatly distressed, and they went and reported to their lord all that had taken place. Then his lord summoned him and said to him, 'You wicked slave! I forgave you all that debt because you pleaded with me. Should you not have had mercy on your fellow slave, as I had mercy on you?' And in anger his lord handed him over to be tortured until he would pay his entire debt. So my heavenly Father will also do to every one of you, if you do not forgive your brother or sister from your heart.
Matthew 18:23-35

Category: What type of parable is it?

The parable is a full length story about the character of the citizens of God's kingdom. At the last judgement they will be judged by their willingness to forgive others in the light of God's forgiveness of them. The story reveals divine grace and measures human responsibility. It features three main participants: a Gentile king, a major official and a minor official. The first forgives the second but the second refuses to forgive the third. This leads to judgement of the unforgiving official.

Context: When and where is the parable's situation?

In the life of Jesus the tale about a Gentile king catches the attention of his Jewish listeners. The story is told in extravagant and exaggerated style. No Jewish king had the power to sell a debtor together with his wife, children and possessions. No Jewish official owed such a preposterous amount. The major official's promise to repay can't be fulfilled and the minor official's promise to repay can be fulfilled. The major official gets what he gave to the minor official. Is Jesus suggesting to some that God is harder than they are when he condemns the unforgiving servant? Is Jesus suggesting to others that God is softer than they are because he had forgiven him previously?

In the life of the churches for whom Matthew's Gospel is written the parable is extremely relevant. The Gospel has five collections of the teaching of Jesus about the divine domain's conduct (Matthew 5 to 7), commission (Matthew 10), comparisons (Matthew 13), community (Matthew 18), and completion (Matthew 24 to 25). The parable of the unforgiving servant speaks directly to the communities of the followers of Jesus about the absurdity of being forgiven so much by God yet refusing to forgive our fellow mortals so little. Perhaps the editor of Matthew is suggesting that his readers should move from a quantitative measure (*How often should I forgive? As many as seven times?*) to a qualitative measure (*Should you not have had mercy on your fellow slave, as I had mercy on you?*) in verses 21 and 33.

Content: How is the parable to be understood?

The parable commences with a merciful settling of accounts. A wealthy, powerful and ruthless king deals with a major official who owes him *ten thousand talents*. According to the definitive Greek-English lexicon, the Tyrian talent was worth 6,000 drachmas or denarii. A drachma or a denarius, a Roman silver coin, was a worker's average daily wage. This means that the amount of *ten thousand talents* is equal to sixty million drachmas or denarii. A day labourer would need to work sixty million days to pay off the debt. If we assume that a major official could repay the debt at an extraordinary rate of ten talents (or sixty thousand denarii) a year it would still take him a thousand years to repay the debt.[1]

The king threatens to sell the official, with all that he has, into slavery. Astonishingly, the king hears the official's impossible plea, *Have patience with me, and I will pay you everything*. How could anyone pay off such a debt? Amazingly, the king has mercy and cancels the debt. What a merciful reckoning! An unlikely character, a Gentile king, has pity and reflects the compassion of God.

The parable continues with an unmerciful settling of accounts. The forgiven man now proves to be unforgiving. He finds one of his fellow officials, probably a minor official, who owes him *a hundred denarii*. As we have noted, a denarius was a worker's average daily wage. The major official threatens the

---

[1] Bauer, Danker, Arndt, & Gingrich, *A Greek-English Lexicon of the New Testament and Other Early Christian Literature. Third edition* (University of Chicago Press, 2000) p. 988.

minor official, who makes a similar plea: *Have patience with me, and I will pay you.* However, the superior official quickly refuses and savagely throws the inferior official into a debtors' prison. What an unmerciful reckoning! Whereas the major official had been forgiven a huge debt, the minor official is not even given the chance to repay a small debt, let alone forgiven such a paltry sum.

The parable concludes with an indignant settling of accounts. When the fellow officials see what has happened they are extremely upset and report to the king. He is no longer compassionate but furious. He may have had a soft spot when he forgave the major official, but now he proves that he is not a soft touch because of what has happened to the minor official. The king hands the unforgiving man over to the torturers who pressure his relatives to pay money to alleviate the conditions in the debtors' prison. The culprit suffers the indignity of losing forgiveness, getting back the debt with no prospect of repaying ten thousand talents, and facing lifelong torture. What an indignant reckoning! As the king said to him, *You wicked slave! I forgave you all that debt because you pleaded with me. Should you not have had mercy on your fellow slave, as I had mercy on you?*

Connection: Why does the parable apply now as it did then?

The parable of the unforgiving servant has its funny side. Is God really like that? A Gentile king could be nasty, but this king shows good humour in forgiving a debt of outlandish proportions. Is this God in heavy disguise? Behind the figure of the king is God who speaks his words of grace and mercy in the life and work of Jesus. *And out of pity for him, the lord of that slave released him and forgave him the debt.*

The parable has its unfunny side. Are people really like that? Someone is forgiven so much and then does not forgive another so little. Do we recognise within ourselves the darkness of failing to treat others as we would like to be treated? Behind the figure of the debtor is the person who hears the message of Jesus about the demand of God. *Should you not have had mercy on your fellow slave, as I had mercy on you?*

The parable has a very serious warning. As Joachim Jeremias says, the parable is about the last judgement; it combines exhortation and warning. God gives us the offer of forgiveness, a gift of mercy beyond asking or imagining. But God will revoke the forgiveness of sin if we do not share the forgiveness we have experienced with others. *So my heavenly Father will also do to every one of you, if you do not forgive your brother or sister from your heart.*

Craig Blomberg tells the story of a World Vision president who met a woman named Mary in a home for paralysed people in Lebanon. She had suffered in one day the slaughter of thirty-three relatives during the civil war of the 1980s. Druze militia offered her the opportunity to renounce Christ. When she refused, she was shot and left for dead with a cross carved on her chest by a soldier's knife. Next day she was found and given medical treatment. Although she had become a quadriplegic, she told the World Vision leader, 'I have forgiven my enemies because Christ has forgiven me. I would like to tell the man who hurt me that I forgive him too.'

Prayer

Our Creating and Redeeming God, forgive us the wrong we have done, as we also have forgiven those who have done wrong to us. If we forgive others their wrongs, you, our heavenly Father, will also forgive us; but if we do not forgive others, neither will you forgive our wrongs. We pray in the name of Jesus who prayed, "Father, forgive them; for they do not know what they are doing." Amen.

Discussion

1. How does the parable of the unforgiving servant broaden our knowledge of the kingdom of God?
2. Why did Jesus originally tell the parable of the unforgiving servant?
3. What is an application of the parable of the unforgiving servant in the twenty-first century?

5 THE LABOURERS IN THE VINEYARD

For the kingdom of heaven is like a landowner who went out early in the morning to hire labourers for his vineyard. After agreeing with the labourers for the usual daily wage, he sent them into his vineyard. When he went out about nine o'clock, he saw others standing idle in the marketplace; and he said to them, 'You also go into the vineyard, and I will pay you whatever is right.' So they went. When he went out again about noon and about three o'clock, he did the same. And about five o'clock he went out and found others standing around; and he said to them, 'Why are you standing here idle all day?' They said to him, 'Because no one has hired us.' He said to them, 'You also go into the vineyard.' When evening came, the owner of the vineyard said to his manager, 'Call the labourers and give them their pay, beginning with the last and then going to the first.' When those hired about five o'clock came, each of them received the usual daily wage. Now when the first came, they thought they would receive more; but each of them also received the usual daily wage. And when they received it, they grumbled against the landowner, saying, 'These last worked only one hour, and you have made them equal to us who have borne the burden of the day and the scorching heat.' But he replied to one of them, 'Friend, I am doing you no wrong; did you not agree with me for the usual daily wage? Take what belongs to you and go; I choose to give to this last the same as I give to you. Am I not allowed to do what I choose with what belongs to me? Or are you envious because I am generous?' So the last will be first, and the first will be last.
Matthew 20:1-16

Category: What type of parable is it?

The parable about a landowner and his labourers is about the grace of God's Kingdom. The story reveals the good news of Jesus in a nutshell. He talks about God in terms of an employer who may be described as good or generous or gracious, or even eccentric. The parable does not illustrate strict justice or sound economics. It illustrates the spontaneous, unmerited love of God in Jesus for us mortals and our salvation, which is encapsulated in the word 'grace.'

Context: When and where is the parable's situation?

There are two main life situations of the parable of the labourers in the vineyard. Three questions give us the clue to the parable's setting in the life of Jesus. *'Friend, I am doing you no wrong; did you not agree with me for the usual daily wage? ... Am I not allowed to do what I choose with what belongs to me? Or are you envious because I am generous?'* Jesus confronts people who fail to recognise their own envy and greed, boasting and reckoning. Such people also fail to appreciate the opening of God's kingdom by Jesus to others. As Jesus said, *Go and learn what this means, 'I desire mercy, not sacrifice.' For I have come to call not the righteous but sinners. (Matthew 9:13)*

In the Gospel of Matthew the parable concludes with the words, *So the last will be first, and the first will be last.* Before the parable the Gospel records the incident of the rich young ruler (Matthew 19:16-22) and the discussion of riches and discipleship (Matthew 19:23-30). In the process Jesus promises Peter and the disciples that they will receive much more than they have given up to follow him. He says, *But many who are first will be last, and the last will be first. (Matthew 19:30)* At the last judgement the inequalities and sufferings of earth will be put right by God. For the author of Matthew the parable reinforces the equality of reward in the divine kingdom.
me for the usual daily wage? ... Am I not allowed to do what I choose with what belongs to me? Or are you envious because I am generous?' Jesus confronts people who fail to recognise their own envy and greed, boasting and reckoning . Such people also fail to appreciate the opening of God's kingdom by Jesus to others . As Jesus said, *Go and learn what this means,*

'I desire mercy, not sacrifice.' For I have come to call not the righteous but sinners. (Matthew 9:13)

In the Gospel of Matthew the parable concludes with the words, *So the last will be first, and the first will be last.* Before the parable the Gospel records the incident of the rich young ruler (Matthew 19:16-22) and the discussion of riches and discipleship (Matthew 19:23-30). In the process Jesus promises Peter and the disciples that they will receive much more than they have given up to follow him. He says, *But many who are first will be last, and the last will be first. (Matthew 19:30)* At the last judgement the inequalities and sufferings of earth will be put right by God. For the author of Matthew the parable reinforces the equality of reward in the divine kingdom.

Content: How is the parable to be understood?

The parable falls into two parts. First is the recruiting of workers for the urgent task of picking and pressing grapes before the rainy season begins. Recruitment takes place *early in the morning, about nine o'clock* (literally 'the third hour'), *about noon* (literally 'the sixth hour'), *about three o'clock* (literally 'the ninth hour'), and even *about five o'clock* (literally 'the eleventh hour'). The Jewish day began at sunset, but the hours of the day were numbered from sunrise which was about six o'clock. (The Jewish night was measured into three nightwatches.) The length of labour varies among the labourers in this vineyard: twelve hours, nine hours, six hours, three hours, and even one hour! One of the surprising features of the story is the number of hirings.

Second is the reckoning of workers' pay at sundown. The landowner had agreed at sunrise to pay the labourers *the usual daily wage* (literally 'a denarius for the day'). At nine o'clock he had promised, *I will pay you whatever is right*. At noon and at three o'clock he did the same. As late as five o'clock he had hired others whom he described as standing here idle all day. The landowner is a just employer. He observes the traditional law: *You shall not withhold the wages of poor and needy labourers ... You shall pay them their wages daily before sunset. (Deuteronomy 24:14-15; compare Leviticus 19:13)* The landowner tells his manager to call the day workers for payment of their day wages.

An explanatory note is in order. A denarius was a Roman silver coin which originally weighed about 4.55 grams. After the time of Jesus the coinage was debased under Nero and the denarius was reduced in value. It was a labourer's average daily wage.[1]

The landowner begins with the last of the hired workers. Each of the five o'clock group receives *the usual daily wage* (literally 'a denarius')! Apparently the same payment is made to the three o'clock, the noon, and the nine o'clock groups. Eventually, much to their horror, each of the sunrise group receives *the usual daily wage* (literally 'a denarius')! Their complaint is that they have not received sufficient recompense for the duration (*the burden of the day*) and hardship (*the scorching heat*) of their work. The rule of 'end stress' means that the emphasis falls on the end of the story. The landowner's

---

[1] Bauer, Danker, Arndt, & Gingrich, *A Greek-English Lexicon of the New Testament and Other Early Christian Literature. Third edition* (University of Chicago Press, 2000) p. 223.

reply refers to his fairness and generosity with three questions: *Did you not agree with me for the usual daily wage? ... Am I not allowed to do what I choose with what belongs to me? Or are you envious because I am generous?* Yes, another of the surprising features of the story is the equality of wages.

Connection: Why does the parable apply now as it did then?

The tale of landowner and labourers raises questions about justice, sovereignty and goodness. Is life fair and is God just? Does the landowner illustrate God's justice? *Friend, I am doing you no wrong; did you not agree with me for the usual daily wage? Take what belongs to you and go.* The Greek word for *Friend* is a quite unfriendly word for 'friend'. Here it is used by the landowner answering the speaker for the workers who grumble at the wage given to the latecomers. Elsewhere it is used in a parable by the king addressing the man without a wedding garment (Matthew 22:12) and in real life by Jesus to Judas who is betraying him (Matthew 26:50). The use of the word seems to denote disregard and scorn for a relationship with the one who has kept his promise in Jesus.

Who is in charge, the creator or the creature? Is the landowner a picture of God's sovereignty? *I choose to give to this last the same as I give to you. Am I not allowed to do what I choose with what belongs to me?* There is a vast gap between landowner and day labourer just as there is between the creator and the creature. But this does not mean that the sovereign God is uncaring. Far from it. We need only think of God in terms of the waiting father who copes with two different sons in Jesus' famous parable about the prodigal son (Luke 15:11-32).

Does our lifestyle reveal a taker or a giver? Is the landowner a demonstration of God's goodness? *Or are you envious because I am generous?* (literally 'Or is your eye evil because I am good?') An 'evil eye' refers to distorted moral vision, the failure to see things in the way of God who is just and fair, sovereign and powerful, good and generous. Helmut Thielicke reminds us of two things. We shall not be able to see God's goodness with a jealous eye by making insidious comparisons of blessings. We can be certain that God is good if we trust that he cares for all his children beyond all our personal calculations.

Prayer

Our Creating and Redeeming God, speak to us and through us of your justice, sovereignty and goodness. Help us to set high regard on our relationship with you. Help us to treat you as Father and Jesus as your Son. Help us to treat others as we would like to be treated. Let others see in us your fairness, power and goodness. We pray in the name of Jesus our Lord. Amen.

Discussion

1. How does the parable of the labourers in the vineyard add to our understanding of the kingdom of God?
2. Why did Jesus originally tell the parable of the labourers in the vineyard?
3. What does the parable of the labourers in the vineyard say to us in our world?

6   THE TALENTS AND THE POUNDS

For it is as if a man, going on a journey, summoned his slaves and entrusted his property to them; to one he gave five talents, to another two, to another one, to each according to his ability. Then he went away. The one who had received the five talents went off at once and traded with them, and made five more talents. In the same way, the one who had the two talents made two more talents. But the one who had received the one talent went off and dug a hole in the ground and hid his master's money. After a long time the master of those slaves came and settled accounts with them. Then the one who had received the five talents came forward, bringing five more talents, saying, 'Master, you handed over to me five talents; see, I have made five more talents.' His master said to him, 'Well done, good and trustworthy slave; you have been trustworthy in a few things, I will put you in charge of many things; enter into the joy of your master.' And the one with the two talents also came forward, saying, 'Master, you handed over to me two talents; see, I have made two more talents.' His master said to him, 'Well done, good and trustworthy slave; you have been trustworthy in a few things, I will put you in charge of many things; enter into the joy of your master.' Then the one who had received the one talent also came forward, saying, 'Master, I knew that you were a harsh man, reaping where you did not sow, and gathering where you did not scatter seed; so I was afraid, and I went and hid your talent in the ground. Here you have what is yours.' But his master replied, 'You wicked and lazy slave! You knew, did you, that I reap where I did not sow, and gather where I did not scatter? Then you ought to have invested my money with the bankers, and on my return I would have received what was my own with interest. So take the talent from him, and give it to the one with the ten talents. For to all those who have, more will be given, and they will have an abundance; but from those who have nothing, even what they have will be taken away. As for this worthless slave, throw him into the outer darkness, where there will be weeping and gnashing of teeth.'
Matthew 25:14-30

A nobleman went to a distant country to get royal power for himself and then return. He summoned ten of his slaves, and gave them ten pounds, and said to them, 'Do business with these until I come back.' But the citizens of his country hated him and sent a delegation after him, saying, 'We do not want this man to rule over us.' When he returned, having received royal power, he ordered these slaves, to whom he had given the money, to be summoned so that he might find out what they had gained by trading. The first came forward and said, 'Lord, your pound has made ten more pounds.' He said to him, 'Well done, good slave! Because you have been trustworthy in a very small thing, take charge of ten cities.' Then the second came, saying, 'Lord, your pound has made five pounds.' He said to him, 'And you, rule over five cities.' Then the other came, saying, 'Lord, here is your pound. I wrapped it up in a piece of cloth, for I was afraid of you, because you are a harsh man; you take what you did not deposit, and reap what you did not sow.' He said to him, 'I will judge you by your own words, you wicked slave! You knew, did you, that I was a harsh man, taking what I did not deposit and reaping what I did not sow? Why then did you not put my money into the bank? Then when I returned, I could have collected it with interest.' He said to the bystanders, 'Take the pound from him and give it to the one who has ten pounds.' (And they said to him, 'Lord, he has ten pounds!') 'I tell you, to all those who have, more will be given; but from those who have nothing, even what they have will be taken away. But as for these enemies of mine who did not want me to be king over them—bring them here and slaughter them in my presence.' Luke 19:12-27

Category: What type of parables are they?

The original parable behind these two parables has been entitled "the money in trust". Matthew's version of the parable utilises the expensive monetary measure of talents. Luke's version of the parable is in terms of the inexpensive monetary measure of pounds. Talents and pounds will be explained in the discussion of content. The original parable and its Matthean and Lukan variants are all parables of crisis. The focus is on the hour of decision in view of the judgement and victory of God which is starting to be realised in Jesus the man of Nazareth and will be conclusively consummated in Jesus the Lord.

Context: When and where are the parables' situations?

There are two main life situations of the parables. First, in the ministry of Jesus his opponents and his followers are challenged to acknowledge the privilege and responsibility they have to be faithful recipients of the message of Jesus. Will they hear the words of commendation, *Well done, good and trustworthy slave; you have been trustworthy in a few things, I will put you in charge of many things; enter into the joy of your master* or *Well done, good slave! Because you have been trustworthy in a very small thing, take charge of (a number of) cities*? On the other hand, will they hear the words of condemnation, *As for this worthless slave, throw him into the outer darkness, where there will be weeping and gnashing of teeth* or *But as for these enemies of mine who did not want me to be king over them—bring them here and slaughter them in my presence?*

Second, after the crucifixion and resurrection of Jesus believers and unbelievers are reminded that at the second coming of Jesus the final judgement will be a divine assessment of the use of opportunities to serve the Lord. In Matthew, *A man, going on a journey, summoned his slaves and entrusted his property to them; to one he gave five talents, to another two, to another one, to each according to his ability. Then he went away.* In Luke, *A nobleman went to a distant country to get royal power for himself and then return. He summoned ten of his slaves, and gave them ten pounds, and said to them, 'Do business with these until I come back.'* At the end comes the summing up. In Matthew, *For to all those who have, more will be given, and they will have an abundance; but from those who have nothing, even what they have will be taken away.* In Luke, *I tell you, to all those who have, more will be given; but from those who have nothing, even what they have will be taken away.*

Content: How are the parables to be understood?

Most scholars have come to the conclusion that the parables of the talents and the pounds are variants of an original parable about money in trust. The original has been reconstructed in the following manner. A person in authority summoned his servants, gave them each some money in trust, went away, and on his return called to account for their stewardship. Two servants were able to report substantial increases in capital and were highly commended. A third servant had feared taking a risk and simply returned the money intact. He was condemned and his money was given to the most successful trader.

Matthew's version speaks of three servants who are given five talents, two talents, and one talent respectively. Perhaps Matthew is describing how different opportunities are used. Luke's version mentions ten servants being given one pound each, but, by the end of the story, three servants render accounts of their stewardship. Perhaps Luke is describing how equal opportunities are used. The monetary units of talents and pounds are worthy of an explanatory note. A *talent* was originally a measure of weight varying from 26 to 36 kilograms. It became a unit of coinage. Its value was high and varied according to its metallic composition (gold, silver, or copper). In the land of Jesus there were 6,000 denarii to the talent. A *pound*, literally a *mina*, was a Greek monetary unit equal to 100 drachmas. The purchasing power of a drachma varied. At times it was possible to buy a sheep or one fifth of an ox for a drachma. It was possible to purchase a slave for four drachmas.[1] Luke begins his parable with an implicit reference to an incident after the death of Herod the Great in 4 BC. Herod's son Archelaus was heir to Judea, Samaria and

---

[1] Bauer, Danker, Arndt, & Gingrich, *A Greek-English Lexicon of the New Testament and Other Early Christian Literature. Third edition* (University of Chicago Press, 2000) pp. 988 (talent), 654 (pound), 261 (drachma).

Idumea. He travelled to Rome with a view to be recognised as king by Augustus the emperor. However, fifty Jews and Samaritans went to Rome to protest against Archelaus. As a result he was given the lesser rank of ethnarch. The first century audience would notice the similarity. *A nobleman went to a distant country to get royal power for himself and then return ... But the citizens of his country hated him and sent a delegation after him, saying, 'We do not want this man to rule over us.'*

Matthew and Luke conclude their parables in colourful and differing ways. Matthew says, *As for this worthless slave, throw him into the outer darkness, where there will be weeping and gnashing of teeth.* One is reminded of the judgement of the merciless in the story of the sheep and the goats, *You that are accursed, depart from me into the eternal fire prepared for the devil and his angels ... And these will go away into eternal punishment ... (Matthew 25:41, 46)* On the other hand, Luke says, *But as for these enemies of mine who did not want me to be king over them—bring them here and slaughter them in my presence.* One thinks of the return and revenge of Archelaus upon his enemies. In the infancy narrative of Matthew it is said, *Joseph ... took the child and his mother, and went to the land of Israel. But when he heard that Archelaus was ruling over Judea in place of his father Herod, he was afraid to go there. (Matthew 2:21-22)*

Connection: Why do the parables apply now as they did then?

What is faith? In the present it can be interpreted as taking calculated risks and being adventurous, or playing it safe and following the rules. In both versions the first two servants are adventurous and look outward. According to Matthew, *The one who had received the five talents went off at once and traded with them, and made five more talents. In the same way, the one who had the two talents made two more talents.* According to Luke, *The first came forward and said, 'Lord, your pound has made ten more pounds.' ... Then the second came, saying, 'Lord, your pound has made five pounds.'*

In both versions the last servant risks nothing and looks inward. According to Matthew, *But the one who had received the one talent went off and dug a hole in the ground and hid his master's money.* According to Luke, *Then the other came, saying, 'Lord, here is your pound. I wrapped it up in a piece of cloth.'*

What is hope? The first two servants look forward to a positive future. They are both hopeful. In Matthew, *Well done, good and trustworthy slave; you have been trustworthy in a few things, I will put you in charge of many things; enter into the joy of your master.* In Luke, the first is told, *Because you have been trustworthy in a very small thing, take charge of ten cities* and the second is told, *And you, rule over five cities.* The last servant faces a negative future. He is hopeless. In Matthew, *As for this worthless slave, throw him into the outer darkness, where there will be weeping and gnashing of teeth.* In Luke, *But as for these enemies of mine who did not want me to be king over them—bring them here and slaughter them in my presence.*

Faith and hope are connected with a principle of life. In Matthew, *For to all those who have, more will be given, and they will have an abundance; but from those who have nothing, even what they have will be taken away.* In Luke, *I tell you, to all those who have, more will be given; but from those who have nothing, even what they have will be taken away.* Someone who possesses physical or intellectual or spiritual capacity will enlarge that capacity by experience, while someone who has none will decline into a worse condition as time goes by. Every one of us has God's free gifts available to us. They are either an increasing or decreasing asset according to our response. We either use them or lose them.

Prayer

Our Creating and Redeeming God, enable us to use our talent or pound with faith and hope. Help us to be adventurous and outward looking rather than risking nothing and being self absorbed. Help us to look forward to a positive rather than a negative future. Help us to use rather than lose your gifts, whatever they are, physical or intellectual or spiritual. We pray in the name of Jesus. Amen.

Discussion

1. How do the parables of the talents and the pounds contribute to our insights into the kingdom of God?
2. Why did Jesus originally tell the parables of the talents and the pounds?
3. What is the relevance of the parables of the talents and the pounds today?

7 THE SHEEP AND THE GOATS

When the Son of Man comes in his glory, and all the angels with him, then he will sit on the throne of his glory. All the nations will be gathered before him, and he will separate people one from another as a shepherd separates the sheep from the goats, and he will put the sheep at his right hand and the goats at the left. Then the king will say to those at his right hand, 'Come, you that are blessed by my Father, inherit the kingdom prepared for you from the foundation of the world; for I was hungry and you gave me food, I was thirsty and you gave me something to drink, I was a stranger and you welcomed me, I was naked and you gave me clothing, I was sick and you took care of me, I was in prison and you visited me.' Then the righteous will answer him, 'Lord, when was it that we saw you hungry and gave you food, or thirsty and gave you something to drink? And when was it that we saw you a stranger and welcomed you, or naked and gave you clothing? And when was it that we saw you sick or in prison and visited you?' And the king will answer them, 'Truly I tell you, just as you did it to one of the least of these who are members of my family, you did it to me.' Then he will say to those at his left hand, 'You that are accursed, depart from me into the eternal fire prepared for the devil and his angels; for I was hungry and you gave me no food, I was thirsty and you gave me nothing to drink, I was a stranger and you did not welcome me, naked and you did not give me clothing, sick and in prison and you did not visit me.' Then they also will answer, 'Lord, when was it that we saw you hungry or thirsty or a stranger or naked or sick or in prison, and did not take care of you?' Then he will answer them, 'Truly I tell you, just as you did not do it to one of the least of these, you did not do it to me.' And these will go away into eternal punishment, but the righteous into eternal life.
Matthew 25:31-46

Context: When and where is the parable's situation?

In the life of Jesus there is an ongoing contrast between costly grace, which acknowledges the demand of God, and cheap grace, which ignores the demand of God. We need to ask, search and knock. As Jesus says, *Ask, and it will be given you; search, and you will find; knock, and the door will be opened for you. (Matthew 7:7)* The parable of the sheep and goats distinguishes between costly and cheap grace.

In the Gospel of Matthew a series of parables highlights the responsibilities of the readers: the two slaves (24:45-51), the ten bridesmaids (25:1-13), the talents (25:14-30), and the sheep and the goats (25:31-46). Accordingly, the churches who are addressed by Matthew's version of the good news face the challenge to be faithful, wise, resourceful and merciful followers of Jesus.

Content: How is the parable to be understood?

In simple terms the parable, which is more than a parable, has five components.

First, *the Son of Man comes in his glory.* This has been mentioned previously in the Gospel: *For the Son of Man is to come with his angels in the glory of his Father, and then he will repay everyone for what has been done. (Matthew 16:27)* Who is *the Son of Man*? He is Jesus who will fulfill the hopes and dreams of the Old Testament. *I saw one like a son of man coming with the clouds of heaven. (Daniel 7:13)*

Second, *All the nations will be gathered before him, and he will separate people one from another as a shepherd separates the sheep from the goats.* Who are *all the nations*? Are they all the people of the world, or all people of the world except for followers of Jesus, or all people of the world except for Jews? It is most likely that *all the nations* are all the people of the world. Matthew's Gospel does not restrict divine judgement to non-Christians or non-Jews. The following section equates sheep (on the right hand) with the generous, merciful and giving, and goats (on the left hand) with the self-centred, unaware and uncaring.

Third, *the king* exercises judgement. Who is *the king*? He is *the Son of Man*, Jesus, who is present in the last, the least and the lost! He assesses success or failure to do six works of love: provision of food for the hungry, drink for the thirsty, welcome for the stranger, clothes for the naked, care for the sick, visitation for the prisoner. On the one hand, *the king* will say to the merciful, *'Come, you that are blessed by my Father, inherit the kingdom prepared for you from the foundation of the world.'* On the other hand, the *king* will say to the merciless, *'You that are accursed, depart from me into the eternal fire prepared for the devil and his angels.'*

Fourth, the climax of the judgement of *the king* in each case relates to care for the last, the least and the lost. *The king* will answer the righteous, *'Truly I tell you, just as you did it to one of the least of these who are members of my family, you did it to me.'* Furthermore, the king will answer the accursed, *'Truly I tell you, just as you did not do it to one of the least of these, you did not do it to me.'* Who are *the least*? Some interpreters give a particularist view: *the least* are all Christians or Christian missionaries. Other scholars hold a universalist view: *the least* are the poor and needy. The former view seems forced and restricted. The latter view allows for any who are hungry, thirsty, lonely, naked, sick, or imprisoned, Christian and non-Christian.

Fifth, the destiny of the accursed results from not doing the works of love, and the destiny of the righteous results from doing the works of love. *And these* (the accursed) *will go away into eternal punishment, but the righteous into eternal life.* What is meant by *eternal punishment* and *eternal life*? The parable of the sheep and the goats has profound causes and consequences. It is told by Jesus who keeps the promises of God in the Old Testament. *Many of those who sleep in the dust of the earth shall awake, some to everlasting life, and some to shame and everlasting contempt. (Daniel 12:2)* It is worth remembering that Jesus said, *It is not the will of your Father in heaven that one of these little ones should be lost. (Matthew 18:14)*

Connection: Why does the parable apply now as it did then?

The parable of the sheep and the goats reinforces the delicate balance between God's gift and God's demand. It's almost as if we can't have one without the other. The gift of God is seen at the beginning of the Sermon on the Mount: *Blessed are the poor in spirit ... those who mourn ... the meek ... those who hunger and thirst for righteousness ... the merciful ... the pure in heart ... the peacemakers ... those who are persecuted ... (Matthew 5:3-10)* The demand of God is seen at the end of the Sermon on the Mount: *Everyone then who hears these words of mine and acts on them will be like a wise man who built his house on rock ... And everyone who hears these words of mine and does not act on them will be like a foolish man who built his house on sand. (Matthew 7:24, 26)*

Are we the 'sheep'? They are on the right side, the lucky side in ancient thought. Do we express our knowledge of God by praying for bread for the hungry, homes for the homeless, peace for the fearful, healing for the sick, love for the hard of heart, and Christ for all? Mother Teresa of Calcutta said that she worked for, with, and to Jesus. She served Jesus in the neighbour, she saw Jesus in the poor, she nursed Jesus in the sick, and she comforted Jesus in the afflicted. Shall we hear the positive words of the king, *Truly I tell you, just as you did it to one of the least of these who are members of my family, you did it to me?*

Are we the 'goats'? They are on the left side, the unlucky side in ancient thought. Do we fail to do works of love for the hungry, thirsty, lonely, naked, sick, or imprisoned, Christian and non-Christian? Do we fail to recognise that all human beings are made in the image of God and are brothers and sisters for whom Christ died? If so, we are guilty of sins of omission. How tragic it is to recognise the grace of God but to ignore the demand of God. Shall we hear the negative words of the king, *Truly I tell you, just as you did not do it to one of the least of these, you did not do it to me?*

As the church knowingly, and the world unknowingly, awaits the final judgement, the parable of the sheep and the goats reinforces the teaching of Jesus. In Matthew 24:45-25:30 the three parables of two slaves, ten bridesmaids and talents have said that we are to be faithful, wise and resourceful until the coming of the Lord. The sheep and the goats in Matthew 25:31-46 tell us to be merciful, not merciless. In his sermon on the parable of the tares (or weeds) among the wheat Thielicke quotes the words of the Russian novelist Dostoevski: "To love a person means to see him (or her) as God intended him (or her) to be."

Prayer

Our Creating and Redeeming God, help us to be sheep rather than goats. Enable us to see you in our brothers and sisters. We want to balance gift and demand. You have made us and remade us. You have done so to bring about deeds of love as we work for, with, and to your Son Jesus in the power of your Spirit. This is our prayer in faith with hope. In the name of Jesus we pray. Amen.

Discussion

1. How does the parable of the sheep and the goats deepen our perceptions about the kingdom of God?
2. Why did Jesus originally tell the parable of the sheep and the goats?
3. What is a contemporary meaning for us of the parable of the sheep and the goats?

8 THE SEED GROWING SECRETLY

The kingdom of God is as if someone would scatter seed on the ground, and would sleep and rise night and day, and the seed would sprout and grow, he does not know how. The earth produces of itself, first the stalk, then the head, then the full grain in the head. But when the grain is ripe, at once he goes in with his sickle, because the harvest has come.
Mark 4:26-29

Category: What type of parable is it?

The parable about the seed growing secretly or spontaneously is about the certain coming of the kingdom of God. Jesus is describing the coming of God's kingdom in terms of the whole process of the scattering of seed, the growing of grain, and the harvesting of the crop. Interpreters have focussed on different elements such as the farmer, the seed, the growth, and the harvest. Thus it has been given various titles: the sower-reaper, the confident sower, the spontaneously growing seed, the gradual growth, the harvest, the patient farmer.

Context: When and where is the parable's situation?

In the Galilean ministry of Jesus there are indications of lingering doubts and impatient hopes.

First, the disciple band faced the challenge of doubts about the validity of mission of Jesus. The Fourth Gospel records such a situation. Because of the difficulty of his teaching *many of his disciples turned back and no longer went about with him. So Jesus asked the twelve, "Do you also wish to go away?" Simon Peter answered him, "Lord, to whom can we go? You have the words of eternal life. We have come to believe and know that you are the Holy One of God." (John 6:66-69)* Yet within the ranks of the twelve was a traitor. The parable of the seed growing secretly reminds the reader of the invisible growth of the seed.

Second, the Synoptic Gospels report the presence of an ex-Zealot among the twelve: *Simon, who was called the Zealot. (Luke 6:15)*[1] Accordingly, Jesus warns against the threat of forceful attempts to accelerate by direct action the advance of God's kingdom. *From the days of John the Baptist until now the kingdom of heaven has suffered violence, and the violent take it by force. (Matthew 11:12)* The parable of the seed growing secretly also reminds the reader of the farmer who sleeps soundly and patiently.

Content: How is the parable to be understood?

The parable begins with five verbs in the subjunctive mood: the farmer *would scatter ...* the farmer *would sleep and rise ...* the scattered seed *would sprout and grow*. The subjunctive mood indicates potential. The parable continues with two verbs in the indicative mood: the farmer *does not know ...* the ground *produces*. The indicative indicates reality. The parable concludes with a temporal subjunctive - *when* the crop *is ripe* -

---

[1] The Greek word for *Zealot* is used to indicate (1) an enthusiast, adherent, loyalist, as in *being zealous for God (Acts 22:3)*; (2) an ultranationalist, patriot, zealot, as in *Simon, who was called the Zealot (Luke 6:15)* and *Simon the Zealot (Acts 1:13)*, to distinguish him from Simon Peter. [Interestingly, Tom Wright, *The New Testament for Everyone*, translates the word 'the hothead' in Luke 6 while retaining 'the zealot' in Acts 1.] See Bauer, Danker, Arndt, Gingrich, *A Greek-English Lexicon of the New Testament and other Early Christian Literature, Third Edition* (University of Chicago Press, 2000) p. 427.

and two indicatives of reality - the farmer *goes in* with his sickle, for the harvest *has come*.

Overall the parable is a short story about the scattering of the seed, the growing of the grain, and the harvesting of the crop. At the centre of the parable are two realities: a sleeping and waking farmer, the sprouting and growing seed. The farmer, on the one hand, does know the daily rhythm of Hebrew life: *And there was evening and there was morning ... (Genesis 1:5, 8, 13, 19, 23, 31)* However, the farmer does not know how the seed sprouts and grows. The sprouting and growing seed, on the other hand, is God's deed in its stages: *The earth produces of itself, first the stalk, then the head, then the full grain in the head.* The word translated *of itself* relates to something which happens without a visible cause. The eye of faith sees the invisible cause.

At the beginning of the parable there is the infinitely small act, the scattering of seed. At the end of the parable is the infinitely large act, the reaping of the ripe grain. Jesus contrasts the beginning with the end. What is implicit in the beginning is explicit in the end. God's kingdom is present from beginning to end. It is like the seed being planted, the grain growing, the crop being harvested. God's kingdom comes in the ministry of Jesus. It grows through the mission of the followers of Jesus.

It culminates in the parousia of Jesus. When the Greek word *parousia* is used of Christ, it is nearly always of his Messianic Advent in glory to judge the world at the end of this age. The word is found in Matthew 24:3, 27, 37, 39; 1 Corinthians

15:23; 1 Thessalonians 2:19; 3:13; 4:15; 5:23; 2 Thessalonians 2:1, 8; James 5:7-8; 2 Peter 1:16; 3:4, 12; 1 John 2:28.[2]

God's kingdom while hidden from some is revealed to others. However, the references to the ripe grain and the reaper's sickle reinforce the arrival of the harvest. One thinks of the words of an Old Testament prophet: *Put in the sickle, for the harvest is ripe. (Joel 3:13)* One also turns to the words of a New Testament prophet: *The kingdom of the world has become the kingdom of our Lord and of his Messiah, and he will reign forever and ever. (Revelation 11:15)* The work of God's kingdom will not always be hidden.

Connection: Why does the parable apply now as it did then?

As we contemplate the parable of the seed growing secretly, we can ask ourselves two practical questions: First, how do we sleep? Do we find it hard to go to sleep? Is our sleep interrupted by the cares and worries of our day to day existence? Perhaps the farmer in the parable provides a clue in learning to fall asleep easily or how to cope with interrupted sleep. He doesn't know how the seed sprouts and grows. *The kingdom of God is as if someone would scatter seed on the ground, and would sleep and rise night and day, and the seed would sprout and grow, he does not know how.* But does he recall the promise of the psalmist? *The LORD will not let your foot be moved; he who keeps you will not slumber. He who keeps Israel will neither slumber nor sleep. (Psalm 121:3-4)*

---

[2] Bauer, Danker, Arndt, & Gingrich, *A Greek-English Lexicon of the New Testament and other Early Christian Literature, Third Edition* (University of Chicago Press, 2000), p. 781.

Second, why do we trust? Do we find it hard to believe? Are our waking hours full of plans and programmes filling our thoughts, words and deeds? Do we fail to notice the beauty of the earth because we are so busy? Do we ever wonder if our life is going anywhere? Perhaps the farmer in the parable has a lesson to teach us about faith. *The earth produces of itself, first the stalk, then the head, then the full grain in the head. But when the grain is ripe, at once he goes in with his sickle, because the harvest has come.* God has given him a block of land which, in God's good time, will produce a harvest. The farmer's experience is paralleled by Paul the apostle, *I am confident of this, that the one who began a good work among you will bring it to completion by the day of Jesus Christ. (Philippians 1:6)*

Helmut Thielicke in his powerful sermon on the parable of the seed growing secretly expresses a sense of wonder. He mentions the graveside of loved ones, the horror of atomic war, the meaninglessness of endless imprisonment and the impact of malignant disease. Then he says, "If I had ever dreamed that God was only carrying out his design and plan through all these woes, that in the midst of my cares and troubles and despair *his* harvest was ripening, and that everything was pressing on toward his last kingly day - if I had known this I would have been more calm and confident; yes, then I would have been more cheerful and far more tranquil and composed."

All of this is in the spirit of Jesus himself who said, *Strive first for the kingdom of God and his righteousness, and all these things will be given to you as well. Do not worry about tomorrow, for tomorrow will bring worries of its own. Today's trouble is enough for today. (Matthew 6:33-34)*

Prayer

Our Creating and Redeeming God, your kingdom is like the seed being planted, the grain growing, the crop being harvested. We thank you that your rule has come in the ministry of Jesus, is growing through the mission of the followers of Jesus; and will culminate in the parousia of Jesus. Help us to lie down in peaceful sleep tonight and tomorrow wake in effective faith. In the name of Jesus we pray. Amen.

Discussion

1. How does the parable of the seed growing secretly broaden our knowledge of the kingdom of God?
2. Why did Jesus originally tell the parable of the seed growing secretly?
3. What is an application of the parable of the seed growing secretly in the twenty-first century?

9   THE GOOD SAMARITAN

Just then a lawyer stood up to test Jesus. "Teacher," he said, "what must I do to inherit eternal life?" He said to him, "What is written in the law? What do you read there?" He answered, "You shall love the Lord your God with all your heart, and with all your soul, and with all your strength, and with all your mind; and your neighbour as yourself." And he said to him, "You have given the right answer; do this, and you will live." But wanting to justify himself, he asked Jesus, "And who is my neighbour?" Jesus replied, "A man was going down from Jerusalem to Jericho, and fell into the hands of robbers, who stripped him, beat him, and went away, leaving him half dead. Now by chance a priest was going down that road; and when he saw him, he passed by on the other side. So likewise a Levite, when he came to the place and saw him, passed by on the other side. But a Samaritan while travelling came near him; and when he saw him, he was moved with pity. He went to him and bandaged his wounds, having poured oil and wine on them. Then he put him on his own animal, brought him to an inn, and took care of him. The next day he took out two denarii, gave them to the innkeeper, and said, 'Take care of him; and when I come back, I will repay you whatever more you spend.' Which of these three, do you think, was a neighbour to the man who fell into the hands of the robbers?" He said, "The one who showed him mercy." Jesus said to him, "Go and do likewise."
Luke 10:25-37

Category: What type of parable is it?

The parable of the good Samaritan is attached to the double commandment of loving God and loving neighbour. The well-known story features a man, probably Jewish, who is attacked by robbers on the Jericho Road, left for dead, uncared for by Priest and Levite, but transported by a Samaritan to the care of an innkeeper. The narrative is about exemplary behaviour, boundless love, the compassion of a Samaritan. It may well arise out of an actual incident on a dangerous stretch of the Jericho road. The Samaritan unexpectedly is a model of a true citizen of the kingdom of God.

Context: When and where is the parable's situation?

Historically, in the time of Jesus there is tension between Jew and Samaritan, indeed, an embittered relationship. For example, Luke records that Jesus was going to Jerusalem. *And he sent messengers ahead of him. On their way they entered a village of the Samaritans to make ready for him; but they did not receive him, because his face was set toward Jerusalem. (Luke 9:52-53)* On another occasion at Jacob's well, Jesus asked a Samaritan woman for a drink. She replies, *How is it that you, a Jew, ask a drink of me, a woman of Samaria?* Then the fourth evangelist explains, *Jews do not share things in common with Samaritans. (John 4:9)* It is true to say that the Samaritans' understanding of the Mosaic Law and their religious worship on Mount Gerizim were considered by the Jews to be inferior.

Geographically, from Luke 9:51 to 19:10, Jesus travels between Galilee and Judea via Jericho. Jesus answers a lawyer's questions about inheriting eternal life and identifying a neighbour, by telling this story about travellers going down the road from Jerusalem to Jericho. Jerusalem is 830 metres (2500 feet) above sea level. Jericho is 250 metres (850 feet) below sea level. The winding road between the two is about 28 kilometres (17 miles) long. Jerusalem, of course, was the site of the temple served by priests and Levites. Jericho was the home of perhaps half of the priests. As we have noted, it is quite possible that Jesus is telling a story based on an actual incident about a triad of travellers who encounter a man in distress.

Content: How is the parable to be understood?

Lawyers were experts in the interpretation of the Hebrew Bible. A lawyer is testing Jesus, *Teacher, what must I do to inherit eternal life?* Jesus asks the lawyer, *What is written in the law? What do you read there?* Perhaps the lawyer quotes Jesus, *You shall love the Lord your God with all your heart, and with all your soul, and with all your strength, and with all your mind; and your neighbour as yourself.* Jesus had said so on another occasion (Mark 12:28-34; Matthew 22:35-37). After Jesus' rejoinder, *You have given the right answer; do this, and you will live*, the lawyer seeks to justify himself and asks, *And who is my neighbour?*

Jesus replies with the story of a compassionate helper. An unfortunate traveller on the road from Jerusalem to Jericho is bashed, robbed and left where he fell. One by one three men come by. The original listeners would expect a trio of a priest, a Levite and an Israelite. **Priests** officiated at the sacrifices in the temple at Jerusalem. The priest would be going home after his duties in the temple. He may have feared being attacked by robbers or he didn't want to be defile himself by contact with the dead. He hurries past on the other side of the road. **Levites** were worship leaders in the temple at Jerusalem. The Levite would also be going home after leading prayers in the temple. He probably has a closer look at the injured man but does not stop to help. **Israelites** were full blood members of the Hebrew race. After the priest and the Levite the lawyer and his companions would expect the story to conclude with a lay person of the chosen people. What would a fellow Jew do for the man left for dead?

However, the compassionate helper is most unexpected. The priest saw the fallen man and felt nothing. *He passed by on the other side.* The Levite saw the fallen man and felt nothing. He *passed by on the other side.* The third man saw the fallen man and felt something. *He was moved with pity.* But he is not an Israelite! He is *a Samaritan.* **Samaritans** were considered to be a half breed and non orthodox community in the time of Jesus. They originated in the eighth century BC during the Assyrian invasion of the north when foreign immigrants were brought to live in Samaria. They recognised the first five books of the Old Testament as authoritative scripture and worshipped God on Mount Gerizim (next to modern Nablus). Today the small Samaritan community has a synagogue in Nablus and conducts Passover sacrifices on Mount Gerizim. They are still classed as non Jewish in race and religion by modern Jews.

The Samaritan does something. He gives first aid to the wounded man, provides transport, arranges for accommodation, and even pays the equivalent of two days wages with the promise of more if necessary. He leaves the man in good hands. The Samaritan is a picture of courage, compassion and commonsense.

When the Lawyer is asked to choose the true neighbour in this case, he has no choice but the Samaritan. However, he cannot bring himself to name him as a Samaritan. He can only identify him as *The one who showed him mercy.* Jesus says simply, *Go and do likewise.* Jesus has changed the question! The lawyer had asked, "Who is my neighbour?" After the parable Jesus asks, "To whom can I be a neighbour?"

Connection: Why does the parable apply now as it did then?

Tom Long gives a memorable report about a group of theological students at an American seminary. The group gathered in a classroom for instructions. Each was to record a talk about the parable of the good Samaritan. However, the recordings were going to be made in a building across the campus. Time was limited. They needed to move quickly. On the way an actor had been placed to play the role of a distressed man. He was lying in the gutter. The students were planning to make a presentation about the parable of the good Samaritan. The lecturer wondered what would happen when the students came upon the man in need. Would they be good Samaritans? No, they were not. Most of them raced past the distressed man. One student even stepped over the man's body in his rush to record a talk about the parable of the good Samaritan![1]

Are we like the Priest and the Levite? They had not learned that the exercise of leadership in regular worship is no reason for sidestepping the challenge to respond to the teaching of the prophets: *He has told you, O mortal, what is good; and what does the LORD require of you but to do justice, and to love kindness, and to walk humbly with your God? (Micah 6:8)* Are we like the Samaritan? He had learned that true religion puts into practice not only love for God but also love for neighbour:

---

[1] See Thomas G. Long, 'Meeting the Good Samaritan' July 15, 2007 www.Day1.org The original report was J.M. Darley and C.D. Batson, 'From Jerusalem to Jericho: A study of Situational and Dispositional Variables in Helping Behavior' *Journal of Personality and Social Psychology*, 27:100-108 (1973).

You shall love the LORD your God with all your heart, and with all your soul, and with all your might and *You shall love your neighbour as yourself: I am the LORD. (Deuteronomy 6:5; Leviticus 19:18b)* Note two things. After the lawyer quotes the twin commandments, Jesus says, *Do this, and you will live.* After Jesus tells the parable, he says to the lawyer, *Go and do likewise.* God's kingdom comes where people feel and act like the Samaritan.

The parable is about being a neighbour rather than setting limits to the neighbourhood. Frederick Buechner has a clever piece in his alphabetical collection of a year's readings.[2] He reflects on the lawyer's question: Buechner (I paraphrase his words) imagines that the lawyer wanted a definition like this: "A neighbour (Party A) means a person of Jewish descent who lives within a radius of five kilometres unless there is another person of Jewish descent (Party B) who lives nearer than oneself. In this case Party B is understood as neighbour to Party A and one is oneself relieved of any and every responsibility!" Jesus didn't give a definition, he told a story about a Samaritan.

Prayer

Our Creating and Redeeming God, help us not to be like the Priest and the Levite but to feel and act like the Samaritan. Teach us to do justice, and to love kindness, and to walk humbly with you. Let us be guided by you to ask 'To whom can we be neighbours?' And so may we love you and our

---

[2] See Frederick Buechner, 'Neighbor' in *Beyond Words* (HarperSanFrancisco, 2004), pp. 281-282.

neighbour in thought, word and deed. In the name of Jesus the Man for others we pray. Amen.

Discussion

1. How does the parable of the good Samaritan add to our understanding of the kingdom of God?
2. Why did Jesus originally tell the parable of the good Samaritan?
3. What does the parable of the good Samaritan say to us in our world?

10   THE RICH FOOL

The land of a rich man produced abundantly. And he thought to himself, 'What should I do, for I have no place to store my crops?' Then he said, 'I will do this: I will pull down my barns and build larger ones, and there I will store all my grain and my goods. And I will say to my soul, 'Soul, you have ample goods laid up for many years; relax, eat, drink, be merry.' But God said to him, 'You fool! This very night your life is being demanded of you. And the things you have prepared, whose will they be?' So it is with those who store up treasures for themselves but are not rich toward God.
Luke 12:16-21

Category: What type of parable is it?

The parable of the rich fool is obviously about money. But it is more than that. It provides an example of behaviour to be avoided. The rich farmer is a hard working soul whose focus is a trouble free future. However, his future is shorter than he expects. He is blissfully unaware of the catastrophe which is imminent. The crisis of the kingdom comes upon him and judgement day is near for him. He fails to realise that he must meet his Maker sooner rather than later. He is too concerned with laying up more than ample wealth for himself.

Context: When and where is the parable's situation?

In Luke 12:13-15 before the parable is a dispute about an inheritance. A man asks Jesus to tell his brother to divide a family's estate with him. Jesus answers with a question to indicate that he is not prepared to arbitrate. He warns against covetousness. After the parable is a generalisation: *So it is with those who store up treasures for themselves but are not rich toward God.* It seems to repeat the parable's climax: *And the things you have prepared, whose will they be?* Although some interpreters see it differently, all three things - the warning against covetousness, the parable of the rich fool, the generalised application - are likely to represent an encounter between two brothers and Jesus.

In the Greco Roman world Luke's retelling of the parable would ring bells in two ways. First, the Greek noun translated *greed* in Luke 12:15 combines the verb 'to have' and the comparative adjective 'more'. The definitive Greek-English Lexicon aptly translates the word 'the state of desiring to have more than one's due'.[1]

Second, the words *relax, eat, drink, be merry* in Luke 12:19 would remind the cultured citizen of the Greco Roman world of a popular attitude to life. Similar words are quoted in 1 Corinthians 15:32 by Paul the apostle, *Let us eat and drink, for tomorrow we die.* Neither Jesus nor Paul advocates such a philosophy. The parable of the rich fool is counter cultural in the ancient and modern world.

Content: How is the parable to be understood?

Jesus tells a story about a rich farmer who experiences the gifts of God without acknowledging the Giver of the gifts. His land has an abundant harvest. The farmer asks himself a question, *What should I do, for I have no place to store my crops?* The farmer answers his question, *I will do this: I will pull down my barns and build larger ones, and there I will store all my grain and my goods.* The farmer surmises with a blessed self-assurance, *And I will say to my soul, 'Soul, you have ample*

---

[1] Bauer, Danker, Arndt, & Gingrich, *A Greek-English Lexicon of the New Testament and other Early Christian Literature, Third Edition* (University of Chicago Press, 2000), p. 824.

goods laid up for many years; relax, eat, drink, be merry.' However, the story surprises with an unexpected outcome. God, the unacknowledged Giver, says to him, *You fool! This very night your life is being demanded of you* (literally, 'they [God and the angels?] are demanding your life back from you'). *And the things you have prepared, whose will they be?*

About 180 BC Ben Sira wrote a book in the tradition of the sages. It includes some words which parallel the answer of the rich farmer to his own question. *One becomes rich through diligence and self-denial, and the reward allotted to him is this: when he says, "I have found rest, and now I shall feast on my goods!" he does not know how long it will be until he leaves them to others and dies. (Sirach 11:18-19)* In the parable the rich fool forgets the uncertainty of the time when a person's life ends.

In Colossians 3:5, written about AD 60, Paul urges his readers, among other things, to get rid of *greed (which is idolatry)* . Paul uses the same Greek word for *greed* as Jesus does in Luke 12:15. In the parable Jesus says that the rich fool is guilty of idolatrous greed. The farmer presumes that good harvests will continue *for many years*. He leaves out of account the Giver of the harvest. He is a practical atheist. As the Old Testament says, *Fools say in their hearts* (literally, 'A fool says in his heart'), *"There is no God." (Psalm 14:1; 53:1)* In the parable the rich fool acts as if God doesn't exist.

Connection: Why does the parable apply now as it did then?

Is life all about me? Arland Hultgren notes that the English translation of the parable underlines the focus of the rich man's life and work. The personal pronoun "I" occurs six times and the possessive adjective "my" occurs five times. The identity of the rich man is tied up with his possessions. His preoccupation is not confined to ancient times. There are many salutary tales of modern entrepreneurs *who store up treasures for themselves but are not rich toward God.* Life can lose its way if we forget that "man's chief end is to glorify God and to enjoy him forever" (Shorter Westminster Catechism) .

Alfred Nobel was a Swedish chemist who grew wealthy by inventing and licensing dynamite. When his brother died in 1888, a newspaper mistakenly identified the dead man as Alfred and printed an obituary for the inventor of dynamite. Alfred's unique experience of reading his own obituary shocked him to the core of his being. He did not want to be remembered as the creator of mass destruction. He put his immense wealth into establishing the Nobel Prizes for outstanding accomplishments of benefit to humanity. Unlike the rich fool, Alfred Nobel walked away from idolatrous greed.

Does life always go on blissfully? In life and death we find that the unexpected can happen. The rich fool forgets the uncertainties in life and death. In living and working he expects many years of abundant crops. He doesn't even consider the possible end of his own life. We only need to contemplate the vicissitudes of the modern world to realise the unexpected nature of life and death. Unemployment, death of a loved one, sickness, financial downturn – any and all make us aware that *one's life does not consist in the abundance of possessions. (Luke 12:15)*

Buddy Holly was a Texan rock'n'roll singer who achieved success in 1957 with a series of hit records. He toured the United States, Australia and the United Kingdom with the Crickets in 1958. As a solo artist in a roadshow group he began a tour of 24 American cities in 1959. After a February concert in Iowa, Holly and two other rock singers hired a light plane to take them to a nearby city. They had grown tired of travelling in an unreliable bus. Unfortunately, the plane crashed in bad weather only minutes after take-off. The pilot and his three passengers died. Singer and songwriter Don McLean in 1971 wrote of Buddy Holly's death as "the day the music died". Posthumously Holly influenced such notable singers as the Beatles. Holly was no rich fool. But, like the rich man in Jesus' parable, his life came to an unexpected end.

In conclusion, a retired person may be tempted to say, *'Soul, you have ample goods laid up for many years; relax, eat, drink, be merry.'* Peter Rhea Jones wisely reflects on the challenge of retirement. Before retirement we may be concerned with building up a superannuation nest egg at the expense of developing lasting relationships with spouse, children and friends. The ways of the workaholic do not allow such relationships to bloom and grow. After retirement we may be consumed by thinking of ourselves rather than caring for others. As Jones writes, "Relaxing, eating, drinking, and making merry do not offer an adequate model for retirement." Jesus' words remain relevant before and after retirement: *'It is more blessed to give than to receive.' (Acts 20:35)*

Prayer

Our Creating and Redeeming God, assist us to learn that our life does not consist in the abundance of possessions. Help us to be people who do not store up treasures for ourselves but are rich toward you. As we face the changes life brings, may we follow the way of Jesus in making worthwhile decisions, developing lasting relationships, and caring for others. We pray in the name of Jesus. Amen.

Discussion

1. How does the parable of the rich fool contribute to our insights into the kingdom of God?
2. Why did Jesus originally tell the parable of the rich fool?
3. What is the relevance of the parable of the rich fool today?

11   THE PRODIGAL SON

There was a man who had two sons. The younger of them said to his father, 'Father, give me the share of the property that will belong to me.' So he divided his property between them. A few days later the younger son gathered all he had and travelled to a distant country, and there he squandered his property in dissolute living. When he had spent everything, a severe famine took place throughout that country, and he began to be in need. So he went and hired himself out to one of the citizens of that country, who sent him to his fields to feed the pigs. He would gladly have filled himself with the pods that the pigs were eating; and no one gave him anything. But when he came to himself he said, 'How many of my father's hired hands have bread enough and to spare, but here I am dying of hunger! I will get up and go to my father, and I will say to him, "Father, I have sinned against heaven and before you; I am no longer worthy to be called your son; treat me like one of your hired hands."' So he set off and went to his father. But while he was still far off, his father saw him and was filled with compassion; he ran and put his arms around him and kissed him. Then the son said to him, 'Father, I have sinned against heaven and before you; I am no longer worthy to be called your son.' But the father said to his slaves, 'Quickly, bring out a robe—the best one—and put it on him; put a ring on his finger and sandals on his feet. And get the fatted calf and kill it, and let us eat and celebrate; for this son of mine was dead and is alive again; he was lost and is found!' And they began to celebrate. Now his elder son was in the field; and when he came and approached the house, he heard music and dancing. He called one of the slaves and asked what was going on. He replied, 'Your brother has come, and your father has killed the fatted calf, because he has got him back safe and sound.' Then he became angry and refused to go in. His father came out and began to plead with him. But he answered his father, 'Listen! For all these years I have been working like a slave for you, and I have never disobeyed your command; yet you have never given me even a young goat so that I might celebrate with my friends. But when this son of yours came back, who has devoured your property with prostitutes, you killed the fatted calf for him!' Then the father said to him, 'Son, you are always with me, and all that is mine is yours. But we had to celebrate and rejoice, because this brother of yours was dead and has come to life; he was lost and has been found.'
Luke 15:11-32

Category: What type of parable is it?

The common title for this story of Jesus is the parable of the prodigal son. The English adjective prodigal means wastefully or recklessly extravagant and is derived from the Latin *prodigus*. The son in the parable is someone who has spent his money with wasteful extravagance. The parable has also been given other titles: the father's love, the lost son, the reluctant brother, the compassionate father and his two lost sons. It is a parable of the revelation of God. It shows God's love for the lost. The parable is about the grace of God's kingdom.

Context: When and where is the parable's situation?

The context of the parable is given in the introduction to Jesus' three parables in the fifteenth chapter of Luke's Gospel. *Now all the tax collectors and sinners were coming near to listen to him. And the Pharisees and the scribes were grumbling and saying, "This fellow welcomes sinners and eats with them."* *(Luke 15:1-2)* The parable of the prodigal son is told in the company of *tax collectors and sinners* and *the Pharisees and the scribes*. *Tax collectors* were Jewish toll collectors who overcharged their Jewish clients. *Sinners* were non-observant Jews who failed to keep the Jewish laws. *The Pharisees* were those who separated themselves from others in order to observe their traditions. *The scribes* were teachers and interpreters of the Jewish laws who kept written and oral regulations. (Many of *the scribes* were Pharisees.)

On the one hand, *tax collectors and sinners* hear the good news of a younger lost son who returns to his waiting father. Such *tax collectors and sinners* are being encouraged to repent and experience the love of God who is waiting for them.

On the other hand, *the Pharisees and the scribes* hear the sad news of an elder son who is reluctant to celebrate the safe return of his brother. These *Pharisees and scribes* are being challenged to accept and rejoice with repentant sinners who are entering the kingdom of God.

Jesus tells this memorable story to invite all to experience and celebrate God's amazing grace in the life of sinful and respectable alike. This grace is always transforming. God accepts people where they are, but God does not intend to leave people where they are.

Content: How is the parable to be understood?

The structure of the story is exquisite. In the first half, the younger son leaves home, wastes his possessions, is impoverished, changes his mind, then goes home to his waiting father, admits his unworthiness, is restored to sonship, and receives a celebratory party. In the second half, due to the sounds of celebration the elder son leaves the fields for the home, is told by a slave of his brother's return, is met by a plea of his father, expresses his anger to his father, is assured by his father of his love, hears his father's explanation, and . . . Does the elder son join the party? The younger son has to learn to say 'Father' again and the elder son has to learn to say 'Brother' again. We know what the younger son did, but what did the elder son do?

The younger son had asked for his inheritance early. It's as though he wished that his father was dead. His father granted his request. The younger son received a third of the estate and the elder son will receive two thirds of the estate on the death of the father, in accordance with Deuteronomy 21:17. The second son wastes no time in journeying to a distant land, where he wastes all his money. The first son stays home and waits for the proper time of inheritance.

In the distant land things go from bad to worse. In a time of famine, the younger son becomes desperate and loses his dignity by taking the job of feeding pigs. According to Leviticus 11:7 the pig is unclean for the observant Jew. At this stage he comes to his senses. *How many of my father's hired hands have bread enough and to spare, but here I am dying of hunger! I will get up and go to my father, and I will say to him, 'Father, I have sinned against heaven and before you; I am no longer worthy to be called your son; treat me like one of your hired hands.'* So he heads for home.

The compassionate father is waiting! He sees the younger son in the distance. The old man runs to him and hugs him. He cuts short the younger son's apology by giving him symbols of sonship in a robe, a ring, and a pair of shoes. He also sets in train a family celebratory feast with the command, *And get the fatted calf and kill it, and let us eat and celebrate; for this son of mine was dead and is alive again; he was lost and is found!*

The elder son is not amused! Out in the field he hears strange sounds coming from the house. He asks a slave what is going on. The slave tells him that the celebration is for his returning brother. The elder son is angry and his father comes out to encourage him into the house. The elder son compares his life of hard work with the younger son's wandering and wasteful ways. When he refers to *this son of yours*, his father counters with *this brother of yours*. The father is ever compassionate. *Son, you are always with me, and all that is mine is yours. But we had to celebrate and rejoice, because this brother of yours was dead and has come to life; he was lost and has been found.*

The listeners to the parable include people who are cut from the same cloth as the two sons. Some are like the younger son. Akin to *tax collectors and sinners*, will they be willing to repent and experience the love of God who is waiting for them? Will they learn to say 'Father' again? Others are like the elder son. Unlike *Pharisees and scribes*, will they respond favourably to join the celebration with repentant sinners who are entering the kingdom of God? Will they learn to say 'Brother' again?

Another possible interpretation of the prodigal son is given by N.T. Wright.[1] Understanding the parable in the bigger picture of exile and return, he identifies the younger son with the people of God in the Babylonian exile. In our discussion of the parable of the sower we noted that Wright emphasises the theme of return from exile to explain the work and words of Jesus. In the parable of the prodigal son the theme does fit with the younger son. However, it does not fit with the elder son. As I said about the sower, the theme of exile and return is not the only way of understanding the mission and message of Jesus.

---

[1] N.T. Wright, *Jesus and the Victory of God* (Fortress Press, 1996), pp. 125-131.

Connection: Why does the parable apply now as it did then?

Helmut Thielicke is known for the English title of a collection of his sermons *The Waiting Father*. In his two sermons on the prodigal son, he expounds the parable in a masterly fashion. He recalls the time that he sat his little son in front of a big mirror. The boy enjoyed seeing the smiling image on the glass and then he realised that he was looking at himself. It is like that, says Thielicke, with the story of the younger and elder brothers and their father. We can see ourselves in one of the leading characters. So we may ask, with whom do we identify in the parable: the younger son, the elder son, or the father?

The younger son goes away and loses everything he has. He forgets that everything he has was given to him by his father. He finishes up as a friend of pigs! Well, not quite. In coming to his senses he is willing to say, *Father, I have sinned against heaven and before you; I am no longer worthy to be called your son; treat me like one of your hired hands.* Self-disgust turns to repentance. Homesick, he goes home. He expects nothing from his waiting father. He receives an astounding welcome. *Quickly, bring out a robe—the best one—and put it on him; put a ring on his finger and sandals on his feet. And get the fatted calf and kill it, and let us eat and celebrate; for this son of mine was dead and is alive again; he was lost and is found!* Do we identify with the younger son? He has the option of repenting of sinful ways and returning to his compassionate father.

The elder son stays home and keeps everything he has. He takes his father for granted and overlooks the joy of forgiveness. He finishes up as a self-righteous humbug! Or does he? The story concludes with challenging words of his father, *'Son, you are always with me, and all that is mine is yours. But we had to celebrate and rejoice, because this brother of yours was dead and has come to life; he was lost and has been found.'* The elder son's response is left unrecorded. When the father accepts the younger boy back as a son, is the elder son willing to accept him as a brother? Do we identify with the elder son? He has the option of renouncing his mean spiritedness and embracing his father's transforming grace.

Do we identify with the father? A.M. Hunter tells the story of a modern prodigal. After he turned up in the distant land of another parish he was counselled by the local minister to go home for surely his father would get the fatted calf and kill it for him. The prodigal did as he was advised. Some months later he met the same minister again and was asked, 'Well, did your father get the fatted calf and kill it for you?' 'No,' the young man replied, 'but he nearly killed the prodigal son!' Hunter's story underlines the fact that no earthly father is as loving as the prodigal's father. Is this because the prodigal's father represents God? God is compassionate and caring, encouraging and empowering. And this we know because of the one who tells the story of the two sons, even Jesus.

Prayer

Our Creating and Redeeming God, help us to accept the invitation to experience and celebrate your amazing grace. Whether we are living sinfully or self-righteously, let your grace transform us. We know that you accept us where we are, but do not intend to leave us where we are. Shine your light in our lives to give us the knowledge of your glory in the face of Jesus so that we might reflect that light in our world. Amen.

Discussion

1. How does the parable of the prodigal son deepen our perceptions about the kingdom of God?
2. Why did Jesus originally tell the parable of the prodigal son?
3. What is a contemporary meaning of the parable of the prodigal son for us?

12   THE RICH MAN AND LAZARUS

There was a rich man who was dressed in purple and fine linen and who feasted sumptuously every day. And at his gate lay a poor man named Lazarus, covered with sores, who longed to satisfy his hunger with what fell from the rich man's table; even the dogs would come and lick his sores. The poor man died and was carried away by the angels to be with Abraham. The rich man also died and was buried. In Hades, where he was being tormented, he looked up and saw Abraham far away with Lazarus by his side. He called out, 'Father Abraham, have mercy on me, and send Lazarus to dip the tip of his finger in water and cool my tongue; for I am in agony in these flames.' But Abraham said, 'Child, remember that during your lifetime you received your good things, and Lazarus in like manner evil things; but now he is comforted here, and you are in agony. Besides all this, between you and us a great chasm has been fixed, so that those who might want to pass from here to you cannot do so, and no one can cross from there to us.' He said, 'Then, father, I beg you to send him to my father's house—for I have five brothers—that he may warn them, so that they will not also come into this place of torment.' Abraham replied, 'They have Moses and the prophets; they should listen to them.' He said, 'No, father Abraham; but if someone goes to them from the dead, they will repent.' He said to him, 'If they do not listen to Moses and the prophets, neither will they be convinced even if someone rises from the dead.'
Luke 16:19-31

Category: What type of parable is it?

This parable is commonly called the rich man and Lazarus. The story begins with two men on opposite sides of society. At death they make the transition to the hereafter. There they are still on opposite sides, but with a great reversal. They have both faced the challenge of the hour of death, but the poor man is with Abraham while the rich man is in Hades. And it is too late for any adjustment. The parable could also be called the six brothers. The rich man is concerned about his five living brothers. All six of them face the challenge to respond positively to their Creator in this life. The parable is about the crisis which God's kingdom brings. How are people to utilise the gifts of God? The parable gives an example of non-exemplary financial behaviour in relation to our fellow human beings.

Context: When and where is the parable's situation?

Appreciation of two situations can deepen our understanding of the parable of the rich man and Lazarus.

First, Joachim Jeremias cites a parallel Egyptian folktale about a man named Si-Osiris who journeys to the underworld. The tale concludes with the words, 'He who has been good on earth, will be blessed in the kingdom of the dead, and he who has been evil on earth, will suffer in the kingdom of the dead.' According to Jeremias, Alexandrian Jews brought this tale to Palestine where it became a Jewish rabbinical story about a rich tax collector Ma'jan and a poor scholar. After their funerals the story finishes in the next world with the scholar in a paradise of flowing streams and the tax collector near a stream but unable to reach the water.

Second, Luke locates the parable in a section of warnings about wealth. The perplexing parable of a prudent steward (Luke 16:1-9) is followed by an exhortation to faithful stewardship (Luke 16:10-13). A critique of the Pharisees (Luke 16:14-15) leads to a contrast between the law and the kingdom (Luke 16:16-17). Luke then tells the parable of the rich man and Lazarus. It seems that Luke interprets the parable as relating to the perils of money.

Content: How is the parable to be understood?

The parable has three acts. If Jesus is using an Egyptian folktale and/or a Jewish rabbinical story, he meaningfully makes it his own.

First, the rich man seems to be rich and the poor man seems to be poor. The rich man *was dressed in purple and fine linen* and *feasted sumptuously every day*. Outside the poor man *named Lazarus* was *covered with sores* and wanted to eat the rich man's leftovers. He was in such a bad way that *dogs would come and lick his sores*. It is unusual that the name of the poor man is mentioned in the parable. *Lazarus* is an abbreviation of Eliezar meaning 'God is my helper'. He needs all the help he can get because the word for *dogs* does not indicate household pets but unclean animals.

Second, the rich man becomes poor and the poor man becomes rich. *The poor man died and was carried away by the angels to be with* (literally, 'in the bosom of') *Abraham*. The angels welcome Lazarus as one of the blessed dead in heaven. *The rich man also died and was buried.* He finds himself *in Hades, where he was being tormented.* The rich man in the depths of the place of the dead is contrasted with the poor man in the heights of heaven.

Third, the poor man is rich and the rich man is poor. A dialogue ensues. Seeing Abraham and Lazarus, the rich man says, *'Father Abraham, have mercy on me'*. He thinks that he can tell Abraham what to do. He wants relief by means of Lazarus! Abraham's reply is respectful, *'Child'*. But there has been a reversal of roles for the rich man and Lazarus. Furthermore, *a great chasm* prevents passage both ways.

The rich man raises the matter of his five brothers. He asks that Lazarus may visit and warn them *'so that they will not also come into this place of torment.'* Abraham reminds the rich man that the brothers can hearken to *'Moses and the prophets'.* The rich man begs to differ, *'No, father Abraham; but if someone goes to them from the dead, they will repent.'* Abraham concludes, *'If they do not listen to Moses and the prophets, neither will they be convinced even if someone rises from the dead.'*

The parable warns ancient listeners and modern readers about the failure to use wealth wisely and humanely. The sins of the rich man are not necessarily what he did (sins of commission) but more likely what he failed to do (sins of omission).

Connection: Why does the parable apply now as it did then?

In the following paragraph, the parable is called 'Dives and Lazarus'. Dives is the Latin adjective meaning 'rich, wealthy'. It was used by Jerome in his Latin translation of the Bible. The medieval Roman Church recognised Jerome's version, called the Vulgate, as the standard Bible.

Albert Schweitzer, musician and theologian and doctor, left Europe in 1912 for service as a medical missionary in Africa. Apart from occasional returns to Europe, he spent most of his life in Lambarene, French Equatorial Africa, now Gabon, until his death in 1965. In his book, *On the Edge of the Primeval Forest*, he gives his reason for leaving Europe and going to

Africa. 'The parable of Dives and Lazarus seemed to have spoken directly to us! We are Dives, for, through the advances of medical science, we now know a great deal about disease and pain, and have innumerable means of fighting them: yet we take as a matter of course the incalculable advantages which this new wealth brings us! Out there in the colonies, however, sits wretched Lazarus, the coloured folk, who suffer from illness and pain just as much as we do, nay, much more, and has absolutely no means of fighting them.' Putting aside Schweitzer's time conditioned ways of speaking, we can easily identify the relevance of his words and deeds to our world a hundred years later.

Do we want to be like the dead rich man in the hereafter? Shall we hear the words of Moses and the prophets in the here and now? For example, the words of Micah 6:8 ring true, *He has told you, O mortal, what is good; and what does the LORD require of you but to do justice, and to love kindness, and to walk humbly with your God?* Are we like the poor man? Do we notice the meaning of his name, Lazarus, 'God is my helper'? In Luke 4:18-19 Jesus quotes the prophets, *The Spirit of the Lord is upon me, because he has anointed me to bring good news to the poor. He has sent me to proclaim release to the captives and recovery of sight to the blind, to let the oppressed go free, to proclaim the year of the Lord's favour.* Peter Rhea Jones makes the astute observation that the poor man could well have died undereating just as the rich man could well have died from overeating. As he says, 'both undereating and overeating can be avoided by sharing.'

Kenneth Bailey taught New Testament at a theological seminary in Beirut, Lebanon, from 1967 to 1984. For nine years in that time there was a civil war raging. On his daily walk to work Bailey used to pass a blind beggar. He sold chewing gum out of a small wooden box. Bailey bought his packets whenever he saw him. Generously, he paid double the price and gave the gum to street children down the street. Bailey and the beggar became friends. Although the beggar could not see him, he pictured him in his mind and called him an exalted title. While the civil war waged around them, the beggar remained calm. He was called Abd al-Rahman, 'The servant of the Compassionate One'. The blind beggar reminded Bailey of Lazarus in the parable. As Bailey concedes, in too much of our world the divide between rich and poor reflects unfairness and injustice.

Prayer

Our Creating and Redeeming God, the rich man challenges us to acknowledge our sins against you and your children in thought, word and deed, through negligence, weakness or our own deliberate fault. The poor man reminds us that you are our helper. Whether we are rich or poor, may we clearly hear your message and fulfill your mission through Jesus Christ our Lord. Amen.

Discussion

1. How does the parable of the rich man and Lazarus broaden our knowledge of the kingdom of God?
2. Why did Jesus originally tell the parable of the rich man and Lazarus?
3. What is an application of the parable of the rich man and Lazarus in the twenty-first century?

13 THE PHARISEE AND THE TAX COLLECTOR

Two men went up to the temple to pray, one a Pharisee and the other a tax collector. The Pharisee, standing by himself, was praying thus, 'God, I thank you that I am not like other people: thieves, rogues, adulterers, or even like this tax collector. I fast twice a week; I give a tenth of all my income.' But the tax collector, standing far off, would not even look up to heaven, but was beating his breast and saying, 'God, be merciful to me, a sinner!' I tell you, this man went down to his home justified rather than the other; for all who exalt themselves will be humbled, but all who humble themselves will be exalted.
Luke 18:10-14

Category: What type of parable is it?

The parable of a Pharisee and a tax collector gives examples of a good man's prayer and a bad man's prayer. There is a twist in the story. The good man's prayer is futile, it's a cover up. The bad man's prayer is fruitful, it's an opening up. The narrative is about two men who go up to pray in the temple. A Pharisee is the good man. He is a highly regarded citizen, but he is a picture of self-righteousness. A tax collector is the bad man. He is an object of scorn. However, the self righteous Pharisee is far from the grace of God's kingdom and the truly penitent tax collector is the recipient of God's mercy.

Context: When and where is the parable's situation?

The temple visit could well be based on Jesus' observation of worshippers who went up to the sacred mount. Pharisees were highly regarded by their contemporaries for their observance of the Law in their devotion to God. Tax collectors, on the other hand, were the subject of scorn due to their willingness to work for the hated occupying power of Rome.

It should be stressed that the parable of Jesus is not referring to all Pharisees and all tax collectors. For example, a Pharisee like Nicodemus (John 3:1-2; 7:50-51; 19:38-42) becomes a follower of Jesus, while other Pharisees (John 7:45-49) oppose Jesus. Furthermore, a tax collector like Matthew (Matthew 9:9), also known as Levi (Mark 2:14; Luke 5:27-28), follows Jesus. Luke places the parable in the context of discussions of prayer (Luke 18:1-9) and faith (Luke 18:15-17). Then a rich young ruler is unwilling to trust and obey (Luke 18:18-23), but a blind beggar (Luke 18:35-43), called Bartimaeus in Mark, and a tax collector named Zacchaeus (Luke 19:1-10) demonstrate faith and obedience. Luke by setting the parable in such a context causes readers to think of the links between discipleship and life.

Content: How is the parable to be understood?

Pharisees were 'the organized followers of the experts in interpreting the scriptures (scribes).' Their aim was 'to take the pattern of a pious Israelite ... and to put it into practice ... Some became followers of Jesus Christ and others opposed him and his followers.' **Tax collectors** were Jews hired by Roman holders of 'tax-farming' contracts and had scope 'to exercise greed and unfairness.' They were 'hated and despised as a class'. Furthermore, their continual contact with non Israelites rendered them 'ceremonially unclean' in the eyes of strict Israelites.[1]

---

[1] Bauer, Danker, Arndt, & Gingrich, *A Greek-English Lexicon of the New Testament and other Early Christian Literature, Third Edition* (University of Chicago Press, 2000), pp. 1049 and 999.

The parable contrasts two men: a highly respected Pharisee and an intensely scorned tax collector. Whereas Pharisees would feel at home in the temple, tax collectors may have been a rarity in such a holy environment. This particular Pharisee is standing by himself. (The word 'Pharisee' may be derived from a Hebrew/Aramaic word meaning 'separated'.) He is praying aloud with raised eyes and hands. He is confident of God's acknowledgement as a truly righteous person. How different is the way in which the tax collector prays: he stands afar off, does not look up, beats his chest in anguish .

The contrast between the two is also seen in the content of their prayers. According to the NRSV, *The Pharisee, standing by himself, was praying thus.* However, Hultgren translates the Greek more literally: 'The Pharisee stood and prayed these things concerning himself.' What does he pray about himself? *'God, I thank you that I am not like other people: thieves, rogues, adulterers, or even like this tax collector. I fast twice a week; I give a tenth of all my income.'* In other words, this particular Pharisee is good, not like a hated tax collector. Fasting and tithing are his really good deeds. He considers himself admirable and thinks of others in contempt. His prayer is long on pride and short on humility. The Pharisee denies his need as a sinner.

On the other hand, the tax collector can only pray, *'God, be merciful to me, a sinner!'* This prayer is reminiscent of the psalmist's lament: *Have mercy on me, O God, according to your steadfast love; according to your abundant mercy blot out my transgressions. (Psalm 51:1)* The tax collector confesses his need as a sinner.

What is the result? A Pharisee who exalts himself over a tax collector and is proud of his good deeds has no right relationship with God or mortals. A tax collector who humbles himself as a sinner before God and is aware of his need of mercy goes home from the temple in a right relationship with God.

An historical comment is in order. After the fall of Jerusalem in AD 70, the successors to the Pharisees preserved the Jewish interpretation of the Hebrew Bible at a coastal town called Jamnia. After the ill fated revolt of AD 132-135, the rabbis moved to Galilee and beyond. In time they produced collections of teaching entitled Mishnah (about AD 200) and Talmud (about AD 500). All of this means that the dating of rabbinic literature is uncertain. But it also means that the successors to the Pharisees represent one of two major ways of interpreting the Old Testament. The alternative interpretation of the Hebrew Bible is found in the New Testament.

Connection: Why does the parable apply now as it did then?

Are we like the Pharisee in the parable? Are we self absorbed and judgemental? Do we consider our own good deeds as meritorious? Do we look down on others who, in our estimation, do not live up to our high standards? Perhaps we need to apply to ourselves the words of Jesus in the Sermon on the Mount. *Beware of practising your piety before others in order to be seen by them; for then you have no reward from your Father in heaven. (Matthew 6:1)*

On another occasion it is recorded that Jesus is critical of some Pharisees, *Woe to you Pharisees! For you tithe mint and rue and herbs of all kinds, and neglect justice and the love of God; it is these you ought to have practised, without neglecting the others. (Luke 11:42)* Interestingly, Jesus wants to see both faithful worship of God and practical care for others.

Are we like the tax collector in the parable? Are we humbled and realistic? Do we consider our need of God's amazing grace? Perhaps, like him, we can appropriate the words of the psalmist. *The sacrifice acceptable to God is a broken spirit; a broken and contrite heart, O God, you will not despise. (Psalm 51:17)*

On yet another occasion Jesus has kind words for a tax collector named Zacchaeus, *Today salvation has come to this house, because he too is a son of Abraham. For the Son of Man came to seek out and to save the lost.(Luke 19:9-10)* Zacchaeus responded to his encounter with Jesus by putting past wrongs right.

Prayer

Our Creating and Redeeming God, we acknowledge that we are like other people. We are all made in your image. We are all people for whom Christ died and rose. Father God, as the Maker of heaven and earth, set up your kingdom in our midst. Lord Jesus Christ, as the Son of the living God, have mercy on us sinners. Holy Spirit, as the Breath of the living God, renew us and all the world. Amen.

Discussion

1. How does the parable of the Pharisee and the tax collector add to our understanding of the kingdom of God?
2. Why did Jesus originally tell the parable of the Pharisee and the tax collector?
3. What does the parable of the Pharisee and the tax collector say to us in our world?

PART B: JOHANNINE PARABLES

The Shepherd

Parables of Eternal Life in the Gospel according to John

As we have seen, the parables of Jesus in the first three Gospels compared everyday events with events of eternal importance. They were stories from real life. They challenged his listeners to stop and think about what they were doing with their lives. They focussed on a main idea with figures of speech or comparisons or stories. They commented upon the meaning of God's kingdom in the time and place of Jesus. They were repeated as his witnesses applied the message of Jesus to their time and place in the Roman Empire. The parables of the Synoptic Gospels convey the authentic teaching of Jesus in masterly fashion with perennial relevance.

It has commonly been held by many commentators that there are no parables in the Fourth Gospel. Yet a minority report allows for a different viewpoint. C.H. Dodd in his magisterial study, *Historical Tradition in the Fourth Gospel*, devoted a chapter to 'Parabolic Forms' and identified seven parables. A.M. Hunter in his helpful summary for the general reader, *According to John*, isolated thirteen passages in a chapter on 'The Parables of St John's Gospel.' Both Dodd and Hunter distinguished three types of parables grammatically. First, there were figurative sayings which have only one verb. Second, there were similitudes which have more than one verb, always in the present tense. Third, there were story-parables which have a series of verbs, this time always in the past tense. Whereas the parables in the first three Gospels include all three types, the parables in the Fourth Gospel are the first two types.

When we look at the parables of eternal life in John's Gospel some observations of Eduard Schweizer are relevant. First,

Jesus uses everyday language and connects with his hearers when and where they are. Second, such everyday language of Jesus can only be understood by hearers who get involved personally with the parables. Third, the word pictures in all four Gospels are exaggerated at times and are focussed on Jesus, God's kingdom, or God's kind of life. Fourth, the teaching of Jesus involves continuing education for the believer in the community of faith. Fifth, acceptance of the message of Jesus opens up the future.

Accordingly, it is reasonable to assert that what is latent or implicit in the first three Gospels is patent or explicit in the Fourth Gospel. According to Matthew, Mark and Luke, the kingdom of God starts to live in the followers of Jesus. According to John, the believer abides in someone who is the same yesterday, today, and for ever. The Gospels of Matthew, Mark and Luke tell Jesus' parables about God's kingdom. John's Gospel also tells parables of Jesus, who is the king of God's kingdom and brings God's kind of life.

Like the parables of the kingdom in the first three Gospels, the parables of eternal life in the Fourth Gospel have perennial relevance. As we look at parables told in John's Gospel, we shall draw upon the analysis of C.H. Dodd, A.M. Hunter, David Wenham and Eduard Schweizer. I am also indebted to the commentaries on the Fourth Gospel by William Temple, Raymond Brown, William Hull, Rudolf Bultmann, C.K. Barrett, Alan Culpepper, Gail O'Day, Ben Witherington and Andrew Lincoln. In addition, there are the popular reflections of William Barclay and Tom Wright.

An earlier version of this treatment of the parables of eternal life appeared in my book, *Jesus and Life: Word Pictures in John's Gospel*. Both Synoptic and Johannine parables are truly provocative, dynamic, and creative.

1   THE NIGHT BREEZE

The wind blows where it chooses, and you hear the sound of it, but you do not know where it comes from or where it goes. So it is with everyone who is born of the Spirit.
John 3:8

Category: What type of parable is it?

The parable of the night breeze describes the coming of the life of God's new age. Jesus explains entering God's rule and receiving God's kind of life. The mystery and might of God's Spirit is suggested by the wind which blows in the Jerusalem night.

Jesus had told a parable of the seed growing secretly with the idea of spontaneous and mysterious natural processes: *the seed would sprout and grow, he does not know how.(Mark 4:27)* He now tells a parable of the night breeze: *The wind blows where it chooses, and you hear the sound of it, but you do not know where it comes from or where it goes.*

In the Fourth Gospel, there are four parables of the coming of the life of God's new age: the night breeze (John 3:8), the bridegroom and the best man (John 3:29), the ripe fields (John 4:35-38), and the grain of wheat (John 12:24). Generally, when Jesus in the Synoptic Gospels talks about the coming and growth of God's rule, it is in the Fourth Gospel that he refers to the coming of the life of God's new age.

Context: When and where is the parable's situation?

The first half of John 3 features an encounter between Jesus and Nicodemus. There is a dialogue between Jesus, *a teacher who has come from God (John 3:2)*, and Nicodemus, *the teacher of Israel (John 3:10)*, who is a sympathetic seeker after mature faith. The dialogue in John 3:1-15 is followed by a monologue in John 3:16-21. In the monologue, the Gospel writer highlights the significance of Jesus, who is *the only Son of God (John 3:18)*.

Content: How is the parable to be understood?

The speaker is Jesus, the one of whom John the Baptist testifies, *I saw the Spirit descending from heaven like a dove, and it remained on him.(John 1:32)* Jesus talks about the kingdom of God with a Pharisee named Nicodemus, the one to whom Jesus asked, *Are you a* (literally, 'the') *teacher of Israel, and yet you do not understand these things?(John 3:10)* Jesus explains what it means to enter God's rule and to receive God's kind of life.

There is a play on words: the word for wind is also the word for spirit. On the one hand, it could be translated: "The wind blows where it wants, and you hear its sound, but you do not know where it comes from or where it goes." On the other hand, it could be translated: "The Spirit breathes where he wills, and you hear his voice, but you do not know where he comes from or where he goes."

Each translation taken by itself is wrong. The point of John's Greek is that Jesus means both wind and spirit. It is hard to reproduce the double meaning in English. The Spirit, like the wind, is wholly beyond human control and comprehension. The Spirit, the wind of God, breathes into this world from God. People themselves cannot fathom the operation of the Spirit, the wind of God, but the Spirit is able to bring people within the sphere of his activity and impart his properties to them.

Jesus is saying to the astonished Nicodemus that while salvation is humanly impossible it is divinely possible. Salvation means new life in Christ. This is a case of transformation, not just information. *So it is with everyone who is born of the Spirit.* God alone is the source of the Spirit through Jesus. Followers of Jesus can begin to live all over again by the personal power of the Spirit from above. If the wind is real and powerful, so is God's wind, the Spirit, who gives us God's kind of life when we put our trust in Jesus. There are both natural and spiritual processes which are spontaneous and mysterious.

Christianity is not only something to be discussed, it is also something to be experienced. Jesus challenges us not to wait till we know the source of the wind of the Spirit before we let the Spirit refresh and renew us. Jesus encourages us not to wait till we know the destination of the wind of the Spirit before we set our sails on life's ocean. The Spirit empowers believers in Jesus.

In summary, as he talks about the kingdom of God with a Pharisee named Nicodemus, Jesus explains entering God's rule and receiving God's kind of life. The point of John's Greek is that Jesus means both wind and spirit. Jesus is saying that salvation is humanly impossible but divinely possible. If the wind is real and powerful so is God's wind, the Spirit, who gives us God's kind of life by faith. The Spirit empowers believers in Jesus.

Connection: Why does the parable apply now as it did then?

Long ago a group of young students heard a tape recording of a sermon delivered by Professor James S. Stewart, in which he said, 'Listen to the wind, Nicodemus! Listen to the wind! You can hear its sound - the night is full of it, hark to it in the tops of the trees - but where it has come from and where it is going no-one knows.' The sermon was based on the conversation in John 3. The impact of Stewart's exposition of the words of Jesus remains fresh to this day.

Our answers to three questions may suggest applications of the parable of the night breeze to our time and place.

First, why do we sometimes stubbornly resist a personal transformation like Nicodemus? Change can be a painful process. Shock and disbelief, feelings of insecurity, physical symptoms, feelings of guilt and panic, outbursts of anger and frustration, and idealisation of the past can all be negative features for someone who is reluctant to change. However, on the long road of change there are positive features of realism, attitude, acceptance, and action.

Second, how can habits of a lifetime be changed in a time of decision? William Barclay tells the story of a drunken and immoral worker who was converted to Christ. His workmates made life hard for him. They asked him, 'Surely you can't believe in miracles. You really don't believe that Jesus turned water into wine, do you?' He replied, 'I don't know whether Jesus turned water into wine when he was in Palestine, but I do know that in my home he has turned beer into furniture!'

Third, is a new start possible apart from Jesus' life and message? Over a century ago William James identified conversion as a gradual or sudden process by which a divided self, consciously wrong, inferior, and unhappy became consciously right, superior, and happy as a result of a firmer grasp of religious realities.

Prayer

Our Creating and Redeeming God, you are Lord of life and new life. Let the Spirit of Jesus bring your changing power into our lives as we believe. Thank you for opportunities to serve you and help us to make the most of these opportunities. Remind us daily about the coming and growth of your rule, about the coming of the life of your new age in Jesus Christ our Lord. Amen.

Discussion

1. How does the parable of the night breeze contribute to our insights into the life of God's new age?
2. Why did Jesus originally tell the parable of the night breeze?
3. What is the relevance of the parable of the night breeze today?

2 THE BRIDEGROOM AND THE BEST MAN

He who has the bride is the bridegroom. The friend of the bridegroom, who stands and hears him, rejoices greatly at the bridegroom's voice.
John 3:29

Category: What type of parable is it?

The parable of the bridegroom and the best man is about the coming of the life of God's new age in the person of Jesus.

It is likely that the idea of the Messiah as the coming bridegroom of God's people developed naturally. In the Old Testament God is pictured as the husband of his people. For example, *I will take you for my wife in righteousness and in justice, in steadfast love, and in mercy.(Hosea 2:19)* In the Synoptic Gospels Jesus speaks in terms of a wedding. *The wedding guests cannot fast while the bridegroom is with them, can they? As long as they have the bridegroom with them, they cannot fast. The days will come when the bridegroom is taken away from them, and then they will fast on that day.(Mark 2:19-20)* In John's Gospel John the Baptist raises the possibility of Jesus as the bridegroom of God's people and of himself as the best man at the wedding.

John the Baptist, the best man, gladly gives way to Jesus the Messiah, the bridegroom, who brings us God's kind of life.

Context: When and where is the parable's situation?

The second half of John 3 features a dialogue between John the Baptist and his followers (John 3:25-30) and a monologue written by the writer of the Gospel (John 3:31-36). The dialogue is about Jesus, the one to whom John the Baptist had testified, the one who is baptizing, and the one to whom all are going. John recalls that he said, *I am not the Messiah, but I have been sent ahead of him.(John 3:28)* The monologue highlights the importance of Jesus who *speaks the words of God* and to whom God *gives the Spirit without measure.(John 3:34)*

Content: How is the parable to be understood?

The speaker is John the Baptist who had come before Jesus. John is aware that he had prepared the way for Jesus. He is being asked about the success of Jesus. John answers with a parable of a wedding. He makes a comparison between the bridegroom and the best man.

Elsewhere John the Baptist himself had used a genuine picture from real life to portray the coming Messiah. The Messiah is a harvester whose *winnowing fork is in his hand, and he will clear his threshing floor and will gather his wheat into the granary; but the chaff he will burn with unquenchable fire. (Matthew 3:12)* So, in another genuine picture from real life John the Baptist portrays Jesus as the coming Messiah, *the bridegroom*, God's chosen people as *the bride*, and himself as the supporting act, *the friend of the bridegroom*, the best man. *He who has the bride is the bridegroom. The friend of the bridegroom, who stands and hears him, rejoices greatly at the bridegroom's voice.*

One is reminded of the vision of another John, the seer of Patmos, who sees the marriage of the messianic bridegroom and his bride. The bride of the Messiah portrays a new people and a new city, in a new heaven and a new earth: *The marriage of the Lamb has come, and his bride has made herself ready (Revelation 19:7)* and *I saw the holy city, the new Jerusalem, coming down out of heaven from God, prepared as a bride adorned for her husband. (Revelation 21:2)*

At a wedding the best man gladly supports and gives way joyfully to the bridegroom so that attention is focussed on the bridegroom and his bride. Similarly, John the Baptist, having prepared the way for Jesus the Messiah, fades painlessly into the background. The one who said, *Here is the Lamb of God who takes away the sin of the world!* and *I saw the Spirit descending from heaven like a dove, and it remained on him (John 1:29, 32)*, now says, *He must increase, but I must decrease.(John 3:30)*

John the Baptist gladly gives way to Jesus the Messiah, who brings us God's Spirit. John is happy to be a servant who has no wish to displace his master. This lesson never goes out of date.

In summary, the Baptist is being asked about the success of Jesus. He makes a comparison between a bridegroom and a best man. In time the idea of the Messiah as the coming bridegroom of God's people had developed naturally. John portrays Jesus as the coming Messiah, *the bridegroom*, God's chosen people as *the bride*, and himself as the supporting act, *the friend of the bridegroom*, the best man. The Baptist gladly gives way to Jesus the Messiah who brings us God's Spirit.

Connection: Why does the parable apply now as it did then?

There is an old joke told at weddings. People will say that the best man did not get the bride. Of course, this is a play on words. 'Best man' is the way we refer to the chief attendant of the bridegroom at a wedding. In another context 'best man' can mean the best man for a job or a position. In the time of Jesus the best man arranged the wedding feast, brought the bride to the bridegroom's house, and acted as a guard of the couple on their wedding night.

Three issues may suggest applications of the parable of the bridegroom and the best man for us.

First, how can the danger of religious jealousy be avoided between Jesus and his followers? The Baptist is prepared to be the forerunner of Jesus, he does not attempt to take the centre of attention. In the story of Jesus different characters have to learn, as C.S. Lewis once wrote, 'to play great parts without pride and small parts without shame'. Sometimes in church life with pride we seek to play a major role and we are tempted with shame to play a minor role.

Second, how can we be like John the Baptist and insure that people see and hear not us but see and hear Jesus through us? The Baptist's actions are congruent with his words. He is praised for directing people's attention to the life and teaching of Jesus. How different is the following statement of a well known philosopher to a colleague: 'Your actions speak so loud that I cannot hear what you are saying.'

Third, how and why is Jesus superior to other religious and political leaders? Jesus in his time and place was one among a variety of possible leaders such as the Sadducees, the Pharisees, the Essenes and the Zealots. This is even more so in our time and place. We can think of Christian and non-Christian, secular and sacred leaders. We can learn from John the Baptist who joyfully acknowledges the completion of his work in the superior ministry of Jesus.

Prayer

Our Creating and Redeeming God, help us to be humble witnesses to Jesus like John the Baptist. Remind us day by day that he must increase and we must decrease as the life of your new age comes in our Lord Jesus Christ. Help us to play great parts without pride and small parts without shame in the coming of your rule. Let our words and deeds always point towards Jesus. Amen.

Discussion

1. How does the parable of the bridegroom and the best man deepen our perceptions about the life of God's new age?
2. Why did John the Baptist originally tell the parable of the bridegroom and the best man?
3. What is a contemporary meaning for us of the parable of the bridegroom and the best man?

3   THE RIPE FIELDS

Do you not say, 'Four months more, then comes the harvest'? But I tell you, look around you, and see how the fields are ripe for harvesting. The reaper is already receiving wages and is gathering fruit for eternal life, so that sower and reaper may rejoice together. For here the saying holds true, 'One sows and another reaps.' I sent you to reap that for which you did not labour. Others have laboured, and you have entered into their labour.
John 4:35-38

Category: What type of parable is it?

Just as John the Baptist had told the parable of the bridegroom and the best man so Jesus tells the parable of the ripe fields. Both parables are about the coming of the life of God's new age in the person of Jesus.

In the Old Testament the people are pictured as farmers who *rejoice before you* (God) *as with joy at the harvest (Isaiah 9:3)* and *sow in tears* and *reap with shouts of joy (Psalm 126:5).* In the Synoptic Gospels Jesus speaks in terms of a harvest. *The harvest is plentiful, but the labourers are few.(Matthew 9:37; Luke 10:2)* In John's Gospel Jesus tells this parable of the ripe fields in which the harvest is taking place and the reaper is overtaking the sower.

The promises of the messianic age are coming true for the followers of Jesus. They are encouraged to see the coming of the Samaritans out of the town to Jesus as the coming of the heavenly harvest.

Context: When and where is the parable's situation?

As Peter, Paul and Mary used to sing, 'Jesus met the woman at the well.' The story in John 4 sets the scene at Jacob's well and then proceeds to the offer of living water in verses 7 to 15 and the offer of spiritual worship in verses 16 to 26. The woman leaves the well and goes to the town to tell the townspeople about Jesus in verses 27 to 30. The next section in verses 31 to 38 is the challenge of Jesus to his disciples and includes the parable of the ripe fields. The story concludes with the conversion of the Samaritans in verses 39 to 42.

A visit to the incomplete Orthodox Church built over the traditional site of Jacob's well is memorable. The site is to the east of modern Nablus, ancient Shechem, between Mount Gerazim and Mount Ebal. The well is approximately 30 metres deep.

In this locality John 4 reports that Jesus breaks down three barriers: ethnic in verse 9b (*Jews do not share things in common with Samaritans*), religious in verse 20 (*Our ancestors worshipped on this mountain, but you say that the place where people must worship is in Jerusalem*), and sexual in verse 27 (*his disciples ... were astonished that he was speaking with a woman*).

Content: How is the parable to be understood?

The Samaritans expected a Coming One whom they called Taheb, the Restorer. In the narrative a Samaritan woman makes the link between the Samaritans' Taheb and the Jews' Messiah.

I know that Messiah is coming ... When he comes, he will proclaim all things to us.(John 4:25)

After the dialogue of Jesus with the Samaritan woman the parable of the ripe fields is told by Jesus on the return of the disciples from the nearby town. Jesus seeks to teach the disciples that he is active in the work of his messengers. As we noted previously, Jesus had used the same word picture elsewhere. *The harvest is plentiful, but the labourers are few; therefore ask the Lord of the harvest to send out labourers into his harvest.(Matthew 9:37-38)*

Jesus tells the disciples, *I tell you, look around you, and see how the fields are ripe for harvesting.* Jesus is challenging the disciples to lift up their eyes and see the Samaritans coming from the town. The strangers are fulfilling Jesus' words: *the hour is coming, and is now here, when the true worshippers will worship the Father in spirit and truth.(John 4:23)*

Jesus says, *The reaper is already receiving wages and is gathering fruit for eternal life.* The reaper of the harvest is being rewarded with fruit not for a passing season but for life in the messianic age. The harvest is taking place. The reaper is overtaking the sower. The prophets, as well as John the Baptist and Jesus, had sowed, the disciples now must reap. *For here the saying holds true, 'One sows and another reaps.'* The promises of the messianic age are coming true for the followers of Jesus.

I sent you to reap that for which you did not labour. Others have laboured, and you have entered into their labour. The aorist tense (simple past), *I sent*, is spoken in anticipation with prophetic assurance. Jesus treats the future as already present. The disciples are learning that they are links in the chain stretching from the patriarchs, Abraham, Isaac and Jacob, to the parousia, the second coming of Jesus.

Finally, the experience of the Samaritans' faith grows out of the effective witness of the Samaritan woman to Jesus. They acknowledge, *It is no longer because of what you said that we believe, for we have heard for ourselves, and we know that this is truly the Saviour of the world.(John 4:42)* Second hand hearers of God's message through the woman become first hand hearers through Jesus, God's messenger in person.

The account of Jesus and the Samaritans in John 4:1-42 foreshadows the Samaritan mission of Philip, Peter and John in Acts 8:4-25. There Philip goes to Samaria, proclaims the Messiah, and people receive the message joyfully. Peter and John represent Jerusalem followers of Jesus and give the stamp of approval to a Samaritan Pentecost.

In summary, Jesus seeks to teach the disciples that he is active in the work of his messengers. Jesus is challenging the disciples to lift up their eyes and see the Samaritans coming from the town. The harvest is taking place. The reaper is overtaking the sower. The promises of the messianic age are coming true. Jesus treats the future as already present. Jesus and the Samaritans in John 4 foreshadow the apostles and the Samaritans in Acts 8.

Connection: Why does the parable apply now as it did then?

What is the difference between a pessimist and an optimist at a sports stadium? Is it that a pessimist sees a stadium partly empty and an optimist sees a stadium partly full? A rather cynical writer has said, 'The optimist proclaims that we live in the best of all possible worlds; and the pessimist fears this is true.' Was Jesus a realistic optimist?

Three possible connections of the parable of the ripe fields may stimulate our thoughts and actions.
First, are there times when we miss the point of Jesus' words? The disciples are thinking of their lunch: *'Rabbi, eat something.'* ... *'Surely no one has brought him something to eat?' (John 4:31, 33)* But Jesus is thinking of his vocation: *'I have food to eat that you do not know about.'* ... *'My food is to do the will of him who sent me and to complete his work.' (John 4:32, 34)*

Second, how does the picture of the ripe fields encourage followers of Jesus? H.V. Morton wrote of his visit to Samaria in the early 1930s: 'As I sat by Jacob's Well a crowd of Arabs came along the road from the direction in which Jesus was looking, and I saw their white garments shining in the sun. Surely Jesus was speaking not of the earthly but of the heavenly harvest, and as He spoke I think it likely that He pointed along the road where the Samaritans in their white robes were assembling to hear His words.'[1]

---

[1] H.V. Morton, *In the Steps of the Master* (Dodd, Mead & Company, 1934), p. 178.

Third, as sowers or reapers how do we rejoice with fellow believers in sharing the message of Jesus? In church groups there are people with various talents to contribute and various tasks to perform in a range of activities, which are designed for maintenance and/or mission. Upfront leaders come and go to a greater extent than regular members.

Prayer

Our Creating and Redeeming God, give us not just sight but insight as we consider the words and deeds of Jesus. Help us not to miss the point of Jesus' words. Encourage us to see the coming of the Samaritans as the coming of the heavenly harvest not just then but now. Let us rejoice with fellow believers in sharing your gift of eternal life with other people. Amen.

Discussion

1. How does the parable of the ripe fields broaden our knowledge of the life of God's new age?
2. Why did Jesus originally tell the parable of the ripe fields?
3. What is an application of the parable of the ripe fields in the in the twenty-first century?

4 THE APPRENTICE SON

Very truly, I tell you, the Son can do nothing on his own, but only what he sees the Father doing; for whatever the Father does, the Son does likewise. The Father loves the Son and shows him all that he himself is doing ...
John 5:19-20a

Category: What type of parable is it?

In the narrative of John's Gospel the parable of the apprentice son appears in relation to the third of seven signs. The first sign is the turning of water into wine at Cana (John 2:1-11). The second sign also occurs at Cana when Jesus heals an official's son (John 4:46-54). In both cases Jesus is the giver of life. Similarly, the third sign in which Jesus heals a man at a pool in Jerusalem makes the point that Jesus is the giver of life. Accordingly, the parable of the apprentice son is told by Jesus and speaks of enduring love in the life of God's new age.

In the Synoptic Gospels Jesus tells his most famous parable commonly called the prodigal son. See Luke 15:11-32. It has also been called the waiting father. It is a parable of the revelation of God. It shows God's love for the lost. The parable is about the grace and mercy of God's kingdom. Whereas Jesus in the Synoptic Gospels talks about the grace and mercy of God's kingdom, in the Fourth Gospel he refers to enduring love in the life of God's new age. In John's Gospel, there are three parables of enduring love in the life of God's new age: the apprentice son (John 5:19-20a), the slave and the son (John 8:35), and the Father's house (John 14:2-3).

Context: When and where is the parable's situation?

Near St Stephen's Gate in the Old City of Jerusalem is St Anne's Church built by the Crusaders in AD 1140. The church is the traditional site of the home of the Virgin Mary's parents. (The tradition dates from Byzantine times.) After the defeat of the Crusaders the church was turned into a Muslim school by Saladin in 1192. However, in 1856 the building was returned to France by the Ottoman Turks in gratitude for their help in the Crimean War. The White Fathers restored the church to its previous condition. It is noted for its acoustics.

Next to St Anne's are the ruins of the Pool of Bethesda excavated by archaeologists in the nineteenth century. Originally, about 200 BC, in the days of Simon the high priest *a water cistern was dug, a reservoir like the sea in circumference (Sirach 50:3)*. The dual pool supplied water to the temple. During the time of Herod the Great (37 to 4 BC) another pool was dug. The dual pool of Bethesda no longer supplied the temple with water but was used to wash animals on the way to temple sacrifices. After AD 135 when Jerusalem became a pagan city, the healing power of the water was still recognised but it was now attributed to the Greco Roman god of medicine, Asclepios in Greek and Aesculapius in Latin. The definitive account of the excavations is given in a monograph by Joachim Jeremias.[1] Bethesda means 'House of Divine Mercy' in Hebrew and Bethzatha is its Aramaic equivalent. The twin or dual pool had five porticoes or colonnades: four on the circumference and one across the middle. *In these lay many*

---

[1] See Joachim Jeremias, *The Rediscovery of Bethesda* (Southern Baptist Theological Seminary, Louisville, 1966)

invalids—blind, lame, and paralyzed (John 5:3). The sick probably lay in the middle portico or colonnade. All of this is the background to the account in John 5. Here in verses 1-9a Jesus cures a lame man on the sabbath at the Pool of Bethesda. As a result, in verses 9b-18 Jesus is criticised by Jewish religious leaders. In verses 19-30 he makes claims as the Son of the Father that he can give life and exercise judgement. Finally, in verses 31-47 he gives evidence for these claims.

Content: How is the parable to be understood?

After being criticised for healing on the sabbath, Jesus links his work with God's work of creation. *My Father is still working, and I also am working (John 5:17).* The Jewish religious leaders are furious because he makes himself equal with the Creator thus putting himself beyond their jurisdiction.

He continues to discuss his relationship with God by telling the parable of the apprentice son. He equates his work with God's work. He sees himself not acting on his own because everything he does is modelled on what God the Father does. As Jesus said elsewhere, *And no one knows the Son except the Father, and no one knows the Father except the Son (Matthew 11:27).* Only the Father and the Son really know each other.

The parable begins with *Very truly*, literally, *Amen, amen.* Normally the word *Amen* is used at the end of a solemn statement as in prayer. Jesus uses it at the beginning of an important statement and he doubles its use. Jesus is making a solemn declaration. According to the Gospel writer, the relationship between the Son and the Father is like the relationship between the Word and God. *In the beginning was the Word, and the Word was with God, and the Word was God. He was in the beginning with God. All things came into being through him. And without him not one thing came into being that has come into being. (John 1:1-3)*

Jesus is employing a simple picture of a son apprenticed to his father's trade. Perhaps he remembers his time in the carpenter's shop at Nazareth with his earthly father Joseph. After all, he was called *the carpenter's son (Matthew 13:55)*. Jesus is transforming and deepening a simple picture.

Negatively, *the Son can do nothing on his own, but only what he sees the Father doing.* Jesus as a young man in the carpenter's shop would have been an apprentice learning from the example of Joseph. Positively, *for whatever the Father does, the Son does likewise.* Jesus as a young apprentice would have imitated the techniques and processes of Joseph in the family business.

By way of explanation, Jesus says, *The Father loves the Son and shows him all that he himself is doing.* Joseph as a human father would have been known as a just and caring person who loved the mother of Jesus and their children. Thus the parable of the apprentice son points toward unity of action between Jesus and God and complete dependence of the Son on the Father.

Indeed, John 5:19-30 answers two questions in two tenses. First, the question, 'Who is Jesus?' receives an answer. Jesus shares the power of life and judgement with God in the present (verses 19-23) and in the future (verses 26-27). Second, the question, 'What are people in response to Jesus?' also receives an answer. People can hear, believe, and pass from death to life in the present (verses 24-25). In the future all people will be raised, some to life, others to condemnation (verses 28-29).

In summary, after being criticised for healing on the sabbath, Jesus links his work with God's work of creation. He continues to discuss his relationship with God by telling the parable of the apprentice son. Jesus as a young apprentice in the carpenter's shop would have learned from, imitated, and appreciated Joseph. The parable of the apprentice son points toward unity of action between Jesus and God and complete dependence of the Son on the Father. The parable and the words that follow challenge us to believe in God through Jesus.

Connection: Why does the parable apply now as it did then?

Frederick Buechner makes a wise observation.[2] As he considers finding the work that God wants us to do he writes: 'The kind of work God usually calls you to is the kind of work (a) that you need to do and (b) that the world needs to have done.' The parable of the apprentice son implies that Jesus faced this challenge too.

We can draw connections between the parable of the apprentice son and us by asking three questions. First, what are some things which we remember our parents doing and today find ourselves doing? In every day life we often say, 'Like father, like son' or, 'Like mother, like daughter'. I remember a mother

---

[2] See Frederick Buechner, 'Vocation' in *Beyond Words* (HarperSanFrancisco, 2004), pp. 404-405.

wondering aloud why her children were so independent. A friend advised her to look at the children's parents! Second, what tasks does Jesus say that he shares with his Father? In previous times it was quite common for a son to follow in his father's trade or profession. One thinks of a plumbing business founded by a competent tradesman, passed down to son, and then grandson. Each generation won renown for honest work. Third, as criticism sharpened Jesus' self-understanding, has criticism helped us evaluate our work's motivation and effectiveness? In John 5 Jesus was criticised for claiming to share with God the right to work on the Sabbath day of rest and worship. By way of reply Jesus implied that he acted in union with God and with complete dependence on God.

Prayer

Our Creating and Redeeming God, we acknowledge enduring love in the life of your new age inaugurated by Jesus, whose unity of action with you and whose complete dependence on you challenge us to believe in you, to live as agents of your grace and mercy, to imitate the strengths but not the weaknesses of our parents, and to evaluate our performance of tasks honestly. Amen.

Discussion

1. How does the parable of the apprentice son add to our understanding of the life of God's new age?
2. Why did Jesus originally tell the parable of the apprentice son?
3. What does the parable of the apprentice son say to us in our world?

5 THE SLAVE AND THE SON

The slave does not have a permanent place in the household; the son has a place there for ever.   John 8:35

Category: What type of parable is it?

The parable of the slave and the son is a parable of enduring love in the life of God's new age. In the ancient world there were three contrasts between a slave and a son. A slave did not command the status of a son. A slave did not receive the inheritance of a son. A slave did not enjoy the freedom of a son. The new age which Jesus brings gives the believer status, inheritance and mercy as a child of God.

Context: When and where is the parable's situation?

John 8 is about Jesus as the judge of life. The chapter features the consequence of believing and obeying Jesus. Jesus is in the Temple and is speaking to people who have started to believe but are not necessarily going to continue to believe. If they do continue to believe in him, then they will continue in the household of God. If they truly change their understanding of Jesus, then they will change their understanding of themselves.

Content: How is the parable to be understood?

Jesus is saying that a slave is not a permanent member of the household, but a son is a permanent member. His hearers claim to have never been slaves to anyone. They conveniently overlook their ancestors in slavery to Egypt and their contemporaries in servitude to Rome.

Slaves were a common feature in the Roman world, as an indispensable part of the empire's economy. They were subordinate to and dominated by their masters and sometimes suffered harsh punishment, brutal torture, and virulent abuse. Sons, on the other hand, were highly valued. They continued the family name and maintained possession of the family inheritance.

The contrast between a slave and a son is evident in the story of Abraham in Genesis 21. Ishmael, the slave son of Hagar the slave girl, is deemed inferior to Isaac, the free son of Sarah.

The contrast is also seen in an intricate interpretation of Genesis 21 by Paul in Galatians 4. People who misunderstand the purpose of the law at Sinai belong to the earthly Jerusalem, bound in a human covenant, like the child of the slave woman. People who rightly understand the promise of God through Abraham belong to the heavenly Jerusalem, in a divine covenant, like the child of the free woman.

In John 8 Jesus is contrasting the slave and the son. *The slave does not have a permanent place in the household; the son has a place there for ever.* Whereas a slave does not remain permanently in a household, a son does. The point is well made: followers of Jesus possess the privilege of being sons and daughters of God. They can rest secure in the knowledge of the care of the heavenly Father.

Next, Jesus contrasts the slave and the ex-slave. *So if the Son makes you free, you will be free indeed.(John 8:36)* The ex-slave is the one whom Jesus, the Son of God, sets free. Only the Son of God can make the slave into a son or daughter of God through believing in Jesus.

What a difference Jesus makes in the life of a believer! He gives the forgiven sinner a revitalising relationship with God, an abiding inheritance among God's people, and a liberating freedom to face the future with Christ.

One is reminded of the words of Paul: *There is no longer Jew or Greek, there is no longer slave or free, there is no longer male and female; for all of you are one in Christ Jesus. (Galatians 3:28)*

In summary, in Roman times slaves tended to be treated as things, while sons were highly valued. Jews knew the contrast between Ishmael, the slave son of Hagar, and Isaac, the free son of Sarah. Followers of Jesus possess the privilege of being not like a slave but like a son. Only the Son of God can make a slave into a son or daughter of God.

Connection: Why does the parable apply now as it did then?

Kierkegaard criticised the church of his day in a parable. Farmyard geese went to church each week. The goose preacher would talk about the Creator Goose who had made them to fly. But the talk of flying was not taken seriously, with one exception, for the geese were too fat to fly. However, one goose tried to fly and was viewed by the others as weird. Indeed, he succeeded, flew into the sky, and returned to tell everyone about it. But he was ignored. Every Sunday all the geese went to church to hear the same message. They said, 'Amen!' and waddled home. Finally, all the geese were cooked for Christmas dinner, except for the goose who had learned to fly! Kierkegaard's parable can be taken as an illustration of the difference between the slave and the son in Jesus' parable according to John.

Our answers to three questions may suggest applications of the parable of the slave and son to our time and place.

First, what would it be like to be a slave in ancient and modern times? Slavery was not formally abolished until 1833 in the British Empire and 1865 in the United States. Yet it continues in other guises such as enforcement of child labour and second class treatment of women in various countries throughout the world.

Second, what are the differences between being a slave in a household and a favoured child in a family? Parallels of the distinction between a slave in a household and a child in a family exist today. Sometimes the favouritism of parents can be apparent in a family. One child can be treated as important and another as unimportant. At times the treatment and mistreatment of employees can be obvious in a workplace. Workers can be treated as slaves.

Third, what are we meant to be and do as human beings in response to Jesus? Human personality can provide extreme examples. Some people are cases of 'all talk and no action'. Other people are instances of 'actions speak louder than words'. Are we people of word and deed as we seek to follow Jesus? If so, then we may live as highly valued children of God.

Prayer

Our Creating and Redeeming God, we thank you that the new age, which Jesus brings, gives all believers status, inheritance and mercy as the children of God. Lord, we are grateful for the opportunity to respond to Jesus and to be your children. Lord, in all that life brings we are blessed to entrust ourselves to your care as our heavenly Father and to the cause of Jesus who is our trailblazer. Amen.

Discussion

1. How does the parable of the slave and the son contribute to our insights into the life of God's new age?
2. Why did Jesus originally tell the parable of the slave and the son?
3. What is the relevance of the parable of the slave and the son today?

6 THE SHEPHERD AND THE STRANGER

Very truly, I tell you, anyone who does not enter the sheepfold by the gate but climbs in by another way is a thief and a bandit. The one who enters by the gate is the shepherd of the sheep. The gatekeeper opens the gate for him, and the sheep hear his voice. He calls his own sheep by name and leads them out. When he has brought out all his own, he goes ahead of them, and the sheep follow him because they know his voice. They will not follow a stranger, but they will run from him because they do not know the voice of strangers.
John 10:1-5

Category: What type of parable is it?

In the Synoptic Gospels Jesus tells parables of crisis. For example, in Luke 12:16-21, a rich fool fails to realise that he must meet his Maker sooner rather than later. The crisis of the kingdom comes upon him and judgement day is near for him. By means of such a parable Jesus teaches that decisions for and against the rule of God are crucial. To follow Jesus is to decide for him in the crises of life and death. Such decisions are of ultimate and eternal consequence.

In the Fourth Gospel, there are four parables of crisis: the shepherd and the stranger (John 10:1-5), the traveller in the dark (John 11:9-10), the walker at sunset (John 12:35-36), and the woman in childbirth (John 16:21). Each one relates to the crisis of the life of God's new age. People face a crucial choice. Will they be numbered with the world which *did not know him*, or with his own people who *did not accept him*, or with *all who received him, who believed in his name*, to whom *he gave power to become children of God (John 1:10-12)*?

The parable of the shepherd and the stranger is about the crisis of the life of God's new age. The parable contrasts the positive image of the shepherd with the negative image of the stranger. Will the sheep choose to follow a true shepherd or a false stranger?

Context: When and where is the parable's situation?

The first half of John 10 is about Jesus as the shepherd of life. Jesus uses a figure of speech about the shepherd, the thief, and the doorkeeper to make his hearers think (John 10:1-6). Jesus explains himself in two ways. He uses the symbols of the gate, or the door, (John 10:7-10) and the good shepherd (John 10:11-18). The section closes with division among his hearers about his words (John 10:19-21) just as there had previously been different opinions about his miraculous healing of a man born blind (John 9:39-41).

Content: How is the parable to be understood?

Once again Jesus begins with *Very truly*, literally, *Amen, amen.* The word *Amen* is usually at the end of a prayer. By using it twice at the beginning of a statement, Jesus indicates the solemnity of his declaration as he describes the difference between the thief or bandit and the shepherd.

The danger of *a thief and a bandit* who enters a sheepfold illegally probably refers to the dishonesty and violence of religious leaders who oppose Jesus and his followers. For example, the authorities in John 9 refused to acknowledge the reality of the healing by Jesus of the man born blind and thus treated the man harshly and unfairly.

On the other hand, *the shepherd of the sheep* recalls two types of references. In the Old Testament God himself replaces treacherous leaders and says, *I myself will be the shepherd of my sheep ... I will set up over them one shepherd, my servant David.(Ezekiel 34:15, 23)* In the New Testament it is said of Jesus: *When he saw the crowds, he had compassion for them, because they were harassed and helpless, like sheep without a shepherd.(Matthew 9:36)*

It is likely that *the sheepfold* and *the gatekeeper* are just parts of the figure of speech, not parts of the developed symbolism. The gatekeeper admits the rightful entrant to the sheepfold. The symbols of the gate and the shepherd are explained in the 'I am' sayings which follow in John 10:7-18.

Of course, *the sheep* are the people of God for they recognise the shepherd's voice. The shepherd calls his sheep by name. The shepherd also leads them to safe pasture. The sheep follow their shepherd, but *will not follow a stranger* who is to be equated with *a thief and a bandit*.

H.V. Morton described a scene near Bethlehem in the 1930s. 'Two shepherds had evidently spent the night with their flocks in a cave. The sheep were all mixed together and the time had come for the shepherds to go in different directions. One of the shepherds stood some distance from the sheep and began to call. First one, then another, then four or five animals ran towards him; and so on until he had counted his whole flock.'[1]

---

[1] H.V. Morton, *In the Steps of the Master* (Dodd, Mead & Company, 1934), p. 180.

Morton refers to the words of our key text. *He calls his own sheep by name and leads them out ... and the sheep follow him because they know his voice.* Jesus is no thief, no bandit, no stranger. He is the true shepherd who gathers, guards and guides.

In summary, Jesus describes the difference between the stranger and the shepherd. Dishonest and violent religious leaders oppose Jesus and his followers. God is the true shepherd in the Old Testament as Jesus is in the New Testament. The sheep are the people of God who recognise the shepherd's voice.

Connection: Why does the parable apply now as it did then?

In the Australian outback a utility truck, what Americans call a pick up truck, takes the sheep farmer with his sheep dogs to round up large flocks of sheep. The sheep are carted to the wool sheds for shearing or to the abattoirs for butchering. How different were Bible times! In biblical times a shepherd kept his small flock in a sheepfold near his cottage for their milk and wool. Once outside the sheepfold the shepherd went in front of them and called them by name. The sheep followed the shepherd but they would not follow a stranger. The choice was critical.

Three issues may suggest applications of the parable of the shepherd and the stranger for us.

First, who are the thief, the bandit, and the stranger in our world? Today's religions provide some good and creative things such as health care and education, and some evil and vicious things such as 'holy wars', and a very good thing - a concern for our ultimate destiny. Today's religious leaders include the good, the bad, and the visionary.

Second, what does Jesus the true shepherd promise his followers? Robert Frost's 1923 poem 'Stopping by Woods on a Snowy Evening' spoke of life's challenges:[2]
> The woods are lovely, dark and deep.
> But I have promises to keep,
> And miles to go before I sleep,
> And miles to go before I sleep.

Third, how are the sheep to respond to the true shepherd Jesus? A famous logo on some old recording discs has a dog sitting by an old fashioned gramophone with his head to one side listening to the sound coming out of the trumpet of the gramophone as a record is playing. The record label is HMV, 'His Master's Voice'.

Prayer

Our Creating and Redeeming God, we acknowledge that as dishonest and violent religious leaders opposed Jesus, they oppose his followers now. Help us to follow Jesus the true shepherd who gathers, guards and guides. We want to listen to our master's voice. Let us see what is important and what is unimportant, what is true and what is false as we follow Jesus all our days. Amen.

---

[2] See *The Oxford Dictionary of Quotations* (Revised Fourth Edition, 1996), p. 295.

Discussion

1. How does the parable of the shepherd and the stranger deepen our perceptions about the life of God's new age?
2. Why did Jesus originally tell the parable of the shepherd and the stranger?
3. What is a contemporary meaning of the parable of the shepherd and the stranger for us?

7 THE TRAVELLER IN THE DARK

Are there not twelve hours of daylight? Those who walk during the day do not stumble, because they see the light of this world. But those who walk at night stumble, because the light is not in them.
John 11:9-10

Category: What type of parable is it?

The parable of the traveller in the dark underlines the crisis which confronts Jesus and his disciples in the life of God's new age which is inaugurated by the coming of Jesus and carried forward by the mission of his followers. Jesus is the walker by day who does not stumble as the night of his betrayal, arrest, trial, and crucifixion approaches. The followers of Jesus are to be the walkers by day who don't stumble during the night of disloyalty and persecution.

Context: When and where is the parable's situation?

John 11 is about Jesus who is the resurrection and the life. It relates the story of the death of Lazarus at Bethany. Before Jesus and his disciples reach the home of Lazarus, Jesus tells them the parable of the traveller in the dark. Later on Jesus meets Martha and then Mary, the grieving sisters of Lazarus. Finally, Jesus goes to the tomb of Lazarus and the unexpected happens.

Content: How is the parable to be understood?

Jesus and the disciples are facing a crisis for Jesus is in danger. When they learn of Lazarus' illness, Jesus asks them to accompany him to the home of Lazarus which is in Judea. So, at the beginning, the disciples said, *Rabbi, the Jews were just now trying to stone you, and are you going there again? (John 11:8)* At the end, after the unexpected sign of God's power in the raising of Lazarus from the dead, it is said of the religious authorities: *So from that day on they planned to put him* (Jesus) *to death.(John 11:53)*

In the parable of the traveller in the dark, Jesus begins with a rhetorical question. *Are there not twelve hours of daylight?* Jesus wants to make his listeners think. During the twelve hours of daylight there are the advantages of being safe and of seeing the way ahead. Walking securely in the light of day is different from stumbling perilously in the dark. In the time of Jesus, movement during daylight hours was free and unhindered, but darkness brought carefree activity to an end.

Those who walk during the day do not stumble, because they see the light of this world. On the one hand, Jesus is the walker by day who does not stumble as the night of his betrayal, arrest, trial, and crucifixion approaches. Jesus must make the most of the short time which still remains of his life. The ministry of Jesus is not over yet. As Jesus had said, *We must work the works of him who sent me while it is day; night is coming when no one can work.(John 9:4)* On the other hand, the followers of Jesus are to be the walkers by day who do not stumble during the night of disloyalty, like Judas the one who betrayed Jesus when *it was night (John 13:30)*, or during the night of persecution, like the disciples behind locked doors for *fear of the Jews (John 20:19)*.

On another occasion Jesus had said, *The eye is the lamp of the body. So, if your eye is healthy, your whole body will be full of light; but if your eye is unhealthy, your whole body will be full of darkness. If then the light in you is darkness, how great is the darkness!(Matthew 6:22-23)* Sound eyesight brings things into focus but unsound eyesight fails to do so. Accordingly, the eye acts as the lamp of the body in that it gives the body light or leaves the body in the dark. The healthy eye represents being open to God's message. The unhealthy eye is a metaphor for being closed to the divine message. The difference is the nature of *the light in you*.

But those who walk at night stumble. If Jesus and his followers failed to walk in the light, then they would be succumbing to the darkness. Instead of walking securely in the light, they would be stumbling over unseen obstacles in the dark. The reason would have been quite simple: *because the light is not in them.*

As Jesus had to use to the full the short time which remained to him on earth, so followers of Jesus have to do God's work in the security of Jesus' presence before the dangers of opposition or death come. Jesus is saying that we should be concerned to use our time well and to beware of travelling in the dark.

In summary, Jesus is the walker by day who does not stumble as the night of his betrayal, arrest, trial, and crucifixion approaches. The followers of Jesus are to be the walkers by day who don't stumble during the night of disloyalty and persecution. Jesus urges his followers to be concerned about using their time well and to beware of travelling in the dark.

Connection: Why does the parable apply now as it did then?

It is hard for dwellers in modern urban centres to imagine city life without electricity yet our ancestors faced the night time with candles or lamps. They got up at sunrise, worked by the light of the sun, returned home by sunset, and went to bed early by our standards. The contrast between day and night was all too real. To be a traveller in the dark was a hazardous business.

Three possible connections of the parable of the traveller in the dark may stimulate our thoughts and actions.

First, how do we avail ourselves of the light of God? An early Christian writer offered the following comment: *This is the message we have heard from him and proclaim to you, that God is light and in him there is no darkness at all.(1 John 1:5)* To live in the light of God means to live as God's children, to care for each other as people who are made in God's image, and to believe the truth as it is in Jesus.

Second, what are the forces of darkness that most threaten us today? Today's world offers many examples of darkness in which good things have gone bad. For instance, one may think of the misuse of money, power, and sex. Money is a good servant but a poor master. Power is to be used for the good of all, not for self advancement. Sex is a gift of God in a marriage 'till we are parted by death', not 'while (so called) love lasts'.

Third, what does the parable say to a person in crisis? An employee's contract was not renewed by his employers. The troubled worker went to his doctor for treatment of symptoms arising from his uncertain situation. The doctor treated the symptoms but added, 'If I were in your position, I would show them by your performance that they were wrong!' This advice carried the employee through the time remaining.

Prayer

Our Creating and Redeeming God, we look to you for light in our darkness. Transform our lives, assist us to care and believe. Help us to utilise your gifts wisely and well. Let us do your work in the security of the powerful presence of the Spirit of Jesus before the darkness of opposition or the nearness of death hinders our effective output. In the name of Jesus we pray. Amen.

Discussion

1. How does the parable of the traveller in the dark deepen our knowledge of the life of God's new age?
2. Why did Jesus originally tell the parable of the traveller in the dark?
3. What is an application of the parable of the traveller in the dark in this twenty-first century?

8   THE GRAIN OF WHEAT

Very truly, I tell you, unless a grain of wheat falls into the earth and dies, it remains just a single grain; but if it dies, it bears much fruit.
John 12:24

Category: What type of parable is it?

The parable of the grain of wheat describes the coming of the life of God's new age. In response to negative opposition from Jewish religious leaders and positive enquiry from Greek seekers after truth Jesus tells the parable of the grain of wheat. It is generally true that without pain there is no gain. But it is specifically true that the death of Jesus is the costly price of making God's kind of life available to all of us. Through Jesus comes the life of God's new age.

Context: When and where is the parable's situation?

John 12 is preparing for the Passover festival at which time Jesus will be arrested, tried, crucified, buried, and raised from death. The first half of chapter 12 follows a plot against Jesus. It mentions his anointing by Mary, a plot against Lazarus, his triumphal entry into Jerusalem, and the request of some Greeks to meet Jesus. Jesus is facing the consequences of the entry into Jerusalem which took place on what we know as Palm Sunday. While religious leaders oppose Jesus, some Greeks out of a genuine quest for the truth want to see Jesus. He responds with the parable of the grain of wheat.

Content: How is the parable to be understood?

This is not the first time that Jesus uses the imagery of nature. The kingdom of God *is like a mustard seed ... the smallest of all the seeds on earth ... becomes the greatest of all shrubs ... so that the birds of the air can make nests in its shade.(Mark 4:31-32)* He compares the productivity of a mustard seed to the coming of Gentiles to God. He also compares the work of a sower to the preacher of God's rule. *Listen! A sower went out to sow ... The sower sows the word.(Mark 4:3, 14)*

In John's Gospel the emphasis moves from the sower to the seed. *Very truly*, literally, *Amen, amen*, indicates the solemnity of the statement. It is generally true that *unless a grain of wheat falls into the earth and dies, it remains just a single grain; but if it dies, it bears much fruit*. But it is specifically true of Jesus. The kingdom of God is concentrated in him. Jesus is saying pictorially what he will very soon say plainly, *And I, when I am lifted up from the earth, will draw all people to myself.(John 12:32)* The death of Jesus is the costly price for God's kind of life being available to all of us. Eternal life is found in the one who is *the way, and the truth, and the life (John 14:6)*.

Just as we cannot really envisage wheat by looking at its seed for the seed must be first buried and then must grow as a stalk of wheat, so the Greeks cannot really see the meaning of Jesus until he dies and rises again and draws all people to himself. The parable of the grain of wheat points to the death of Jesus as being necessary and fruitful. Through his death and resurrection Jesus will become accessible for the Greeks as the dying and risen Lord.

The meaning of the parable of the grain of wheat is seen in a saying of Jesus which speaks of his death, *For the Son of Man came not to be served but to serve, and to give his life a ransom for many.(Mark 10:45)* Jesus is explaining his death, in four ways: voluntary(*came ... to serve*), costly (*came ... to give his life*), sacrificial (*a ransom*), and effective (*for many*).

The influence of the parable of the grain of wheat is evident in Paul's letters when he discusses the mystery of life arising from death at the final resurrection. What is said of Jesus in John 12:24 is said of the followers of Jesus in 1 Corinthians 15:36, *What you sow does not come to life unless it dies.*

The parable is followed by a saying about following Jesus. *Those who love their life lose it, and those who hate their life in this world will keep it for eternal life.(John 12:25)* In other words, those who wish to live in and for themselves will become disillusioned. Elsewhere Jesus says, *For those who want to save their life will lose it, and those who lose their life for my sake, and for the sake of the gospel, will save it.(Mark 8:35)* Those who wish to save their skin will be disappointed. We are to follow Jesus through thick and thin.

In summary, in response to negative opposition and positive enquiry Jesus tells the parable of the grain of wheat. It is generally true that without pain there is no gain. But it is specifically true that the death of Jesus is the costly price for God's kind of life being available to all of us. The parable's meaning is seen in Mark 10:45. The parable's influence is evident in 1 Corinthians 15:36. After the parable comes a saying about following Jesus through thick and thin.

Connection: Why does the parable apply now as it did then?

City folks, and I am one of them, can overlook the processes of the farm and the orchard. We can ignore where the ingredients for our favourite wholemeal bread come from and what happen to be the sources of our morning fruit juices. The grains of wheat are planted and in time they produce the golden harvest. The orange pips and apple seeds are buried and in due course they become the saplings which grow into healthy fruit trees. Country folks will understand better the parable of the grain of wheat.

By asking three questions both city folks and country folks can see the implications of the parable of the grain of wheat.

First, why does Jesus seem to put off the opportunity presented by the Greeks? 'Cometh the hour, cometh the man.' Before he tells the parable of the grain of wheat, Jesus says, *The hour has come for the Son of Man to be glorified.(John 12:23)*. After Judas goes to betray him and before he goes to his arrest, trial, and death, only then Jesus speaks of his hour of glory (John 13:31-32; 17:1).

Second, what is the lesson of the contrast between the single grain and much fruit? In the second century Tertullian declared, 'The blood of the martyrs is the seed of the Church.' He was suggesting that as often as Christians were put to death for their faith, the more Christians grew in numbers.

Third, can we name some people who have followed Christ sacrificially? William Barclay mentions the attitude of a famous Welsh evangelist, Christmas Evans. His friends would tell him to take life easier and to slow down, but he would reply, 'It's better to burn out than to rust out.'

Prayer

Our Creating and Redeeming God, we do not really see the meaning of Jesus until he dies and rises again and draws all to himself in the fellowship and mission of the church. So, we thank you for the death of Jesus which is the costly price for your kind of life being available to all of us. Let us learn to be unselfish like Jesus and so by his grace bear much fruit in his service. Amen.

Discussion

1. How does the parable of the grain of wheat add to our understanding of the life of God's new age?
2. Why did Jesus originally tell the parable of the grain of wheat?
3. What does the parable of the grain of wheat say to us in our world?

9   THE WALKER AT SUNSET

The light is with you for a little longer. Walk while you have the light, so that the darkness may not overtake you. If you walk in the darkness, you do not know where you are going. While you have the light, believe in the light, so that you may become children of light.
John 12:35-36

Category: What type of parable is it?

The parable of the walker at sunset speaks of the crisis of the life of God's new age. Jesus is conscious that his ministry is drawing to a close. He compares day and night. He urges people to believe in him before it is too late. Believers ancient still had time as they listened to Jesus and believers modern still have time in this life, but not necessarily much time, to escape the impending doom, and to become *children of light.* Decisions for and against the rule of God in the Synoptic Gospels are crucial, as are decisions for and against eternal life in the Fourth Gospel.

Context: When and where is the parable's situation?

John 12 is preparing for the Passover festival during which time Jesus will be arrested, tried, crucified, buried, and raised from death. The second half of chapter 12 follows the request of some Greeks to see Jesus and the response of Jesus to their request. It mentions his commitment to his calling in the face of rejection by the people, and sums up his teaching about God. As Jesus says, *Whoever believes in me believes not in me but in him who sent me. (John 12:39)* The parable of the walker at sunset underlines the commitment of Jesus to the reality of God. His followers are challenged to be of like mind.

Content: How is the parable to be understood?

Jesus is in danger for the religious authorities *had given orders that anyone who knew where Jesus was should let them know, so that they might arrest him.(John 11:57)* Lazarus too is in danger. The religious authorities *planned to put Lazarus to death as well, since it was on account of him that many of the Jews were deserting and were believing in Jesus.(John 12:10-11)*

By the time Jesus has entered Jerusalem and has responded to the approach of the Greeks by uttering the parable of the grain of wheat (John 12:24), things are getting very serious. Jesus gives the crowd one last chance to see the light, to recognise the light, to be in the light. He does this by telling the parable of the walker at sunset.

The light is with you for a little longer. Jesus is conscious that his ministry is drawing to a close. He has just spoken about being *lifted up from the earth* thus indicating *the kind of death he was to die (John 12:32-33).* Jesus is reflecting the description of the Servant of the Lord found in the teaching of Isaiah of Babylon. The Servant is *a light to the nations (Isaiah 49:6).* He is to be *lifted up (Isaiah 52:13).* He is *a man of suffering (Isaiah 53:3).* Jesus, the light of the world, is willing to go to his death. Perhaps Jesus is encouraged by the words of Isaiah of Babylon: *Out of his anguish he shall see light (Isaiah 53:11).*

Jesus compares day and night. *Walk while you have the light, so that the darkness may not overtake you. If you walk in the darkness, you do not know where you are going.* In his ministry

Jesus has brought the rays of God's light into a self-centred, uncaring, dark world. As the Gospel writer says, *The light shines in the darkness, and the darkness did not overcome it. (John 1:5)* Beyond Jesus' ministry John's Gospel continues to bring the rays of God's light to its readers so that they may turn from a selfish, hateful, and dark existence to the true light and real life of God as found in Jesus.

Jesus urges people to believe in him before it is too late. *While you have the light, believe in the light, so that you may become children of light.* Jesus is challenging his hearers to choose light rather than darkness. He is giving people the opportunity to believe in the light and to be agents of the light. Beyond his lifetime John's Gospel continues to challenge its readers to *become children of light*, to be guided by the true light and to reveal the true light in their lives. Yes, the apostle Paul who himself turned from darkness to light puts it well: *For once you were darkness, but now in the Lord you are light. Live as children of light.(Ephesians 5:8)*

Those who are believers still have time in this life, but not necessarily much time, to make their decision to get going with Jesus while the going is good, to escape the impending doom, and to become *children of light*. Beware of walking into the sunset!

In summary, Jesus, conscious that his ministry is drawing to a close, tells the parable of the walker at sunset. He compares day and night. He urges people to believe in him before it is too late. Believers ancient and modern still have time in this life, but not necessarily much time, to escape the impending doom, and to become *children of light*.

Connection: Why does the parable apply now as it did then?

In the big cities of our world there are places where it is advisable not to go alone after dark. The same places are probably safe to venture into during the daylight hours. For example, one can walk safely through Central Park in New York City during the day but not at night. Walkers at sunset in such a place are well advised to get going while the going is good, and not let the darkness overtake them.

Three possible applications of the parable of the walker at sunset may stimulate our thoughts and actions.

First, what are some rays of light we have in our earthly lifetime? William Temple wrote: 'It is by trusting in and living by whatever light we have that we become sensitive to fuller light.'

Second, what are some forms of darkness which threaten believers? A prisoner of the Nazis left these words etched on the wall of his cell: 'I believe in the sun even when it is not shining. I believe in love where feeling is not. I believe in God even if he is silent.'

Third, what choices are there for people who consider the words of Jesus about believing in the light? Frederick Buechner wrote a prayer for his dying brother: 'Dear Lord, Bring me through darkness into light. Bring me through pain into peace. Bring me through death into life. Be with me wherever I go, and with everyone I love. In Christ's name I ask it. Amen.'[1]

Prayer

Our Creating and Redeeming God, we thank you that we have received the new life Jesus offers and have not remained lost in the darkness. Help us to walk in the light, and to believe in the light of Jesus all our days. Reassure us that the light of Jesus shines in the darkness, and the darkness never did and never will master the light. We pray in the name of Jesus, the light of the world. Amen.

Discussion

1. How does the parable of the walker at sunset contribute to our insights into the life of God's new age?
2. Why did Jesus originally tell the parable of the walker at sunset?
3. What is the relevance of the parable of the walker at sunset today?

---

[1] See Frederick Buechner, *The Eyes of the Heart* (HarperSanFrancisco, 1999), p. 163.

10   THE BATHTUB AND THE BASIN

One who has bathed does not need to wash, except for the feet, but is entirely clean.
John 13:10

Category: What type of parable is it?

The parable of the bathtub and the basin is about participation in the life of God's new age.

In the Synoptic Gospels Jesus tells parables about the citizens of the kingdom of God. For example, there are two parables about finding the kingdom. They liken God's rule to a treasure hidden in a field and the finding of a very valuable pearl (Matthew 13:44-46). One citizen came upon the hidden treasure of the kingdom by chance, the other citizen was searching for the very special pearl of the kingdom by design. Both became citizens under the rule of God. Both became fully committed to Jesus.

In the Fourth Gospel Jesus calls his followers servants and messengers (John 13:16), disciples (John 15:8), and even friends (John 15:14-15). They are sharers or participants in the life of the age to come. They serve the cause of Jesus, tell the message of Jesus, learn to be like Jesus, have the characteristics of friends who do what he commands them because they know God through him. The Fourth Gospel includes two parables about the sharers or participants in the life of the age that comes in Jesus. They are the bathtub and the basin (John 13:10) and the true vine (John 15:1-2).

Context: When and where is the parable's situation?

In John 13 Jesus begins to prepare his disciples for his departure. The surprise washing of the disciples' feet by Jesus (John 13:1-11) leads to a discussion of following this example (John 13:12-20) and then Jesus discloses his coming betrayal by one of the disciples (John 13:21-30). The parable of the bathtub and the basin is Jesus' response to Peter's reactions to the washing of the disciples' feet.

During what we call the Last Supper Jesus gets up from the table, takes off his robe, assumes the role of a servant, and begins to wash the disciples' feet and then to wipe them. The dialogue between Peter and Jesus is not about what Peter does but it is about what Jesus does. The parable of the bathtub and the basin is a picture of being bathed completely when we turn to God and of being washed regularly as we follow Jesus. As we shall see, this fits well with the Christian rites of Baptism and the Lord's Supper.

Content: How is the parable to be understood?

At Passover time, Jesus displays the fullness of his love for his followers. Only John's Gospel records the footwashing. However, it is in harmony with the portrayal of Jesus in the other Gospels: *But I am among you as one who serves.(Luke 22:27; compare Matthew 20:28; Mark 10:45)*

When Jesus comes to Peter, Peter says, *Lord, are you going to wash my feet?(John 13:6)* Jesus replies, *You do not know now what I am doing, but later you will understand.(John 13:7)*

Peter does not understand that Jesus is the Servant King, but he will understand after Jesus has gone to God the Father.

Peter then says, *You will never wash my feet.* Jesus replies, *Unless I wash you, you have no share with me.(John 13:8)* If Peter does not allow Jesus to be his Servant King, he does not share the suffering and victory of his Teacher and Lord.

Peter then says, *Lord, not my feet only but also my hands and my head!(John 13:9)* Jesus responds, *One who has bathed does not need to wash, except for the feet, but is entirely clean.* Peter has to learn to distinguish between being completely bathed before going out to dinner and having one's dirty feet washed after walking on dusty roads on the way to dinner. The dialogue between Peter and Jesus is not about what Peter does but it is about what Jesus does.

Jesus concludes, *And you are clean, though not all of you.(John 13:10)* As the Gospel writer explains, *For he knew who was to betray him; for this reason he said, 'Not all of you are clean.' (John 13:11)* Except for the betrayer, all the other disciples are clean because by God's grace they have made decisive commitments to be followers of their Servant King, and because, day by day, they continue to grow by being helped by Jesus and come to know him better. So then, the parable of the bathtub and the basin is a picture of being bathed completely when we turn to God and of being washed regularly as we follow Jesus.

This fits well with the early Christian rites of initiation, baptism, and of continuation, the Lord's Supper. Baptism in the New Testament is a symbol of purification, identification, and incorporation. Baptism is a sign of being cleansed and forgiven, of belonging to the people of God, and of joining the body of Christ. The Lord's Supper in the New Testament has past, present, and future significance. The Lord's Supper looks back to the death of Jesus on our behalf, enriches our experience of the presence of Jesus in our lives, and looks forward to the coming of Jesus as our king.

Connection: Why does the parable apply now as it did then?

Sometimes we say that someone is throwing out the baby with the bathwater. This is a colloquial way of saying that someone is tossing out what is of value along with what is considered to be rubbish. There may be occasions when someone makes an erroneous estimation of what is to be valued and what is to be considered rubbish. As we have seen, Simon Peter's reactions to this surprising act by Jesus turn out to be over reactions and lay him open to the charge of throwing out the baby with the bathwater.

Three questions may suggest applications of the parable of the bathtub and the basin for us. First, how can we spell out the picture of the bathtub as a decisive cleansing? In John's Gospel Jesus says to the disciples, *You have already been cleansed by the word that I have spoken to you.(John 15:3)* In John's First Letter the writer says, *The blood of Jesus his* (God's) *Son cleanses us from all sin.(1 John 1:7)*

Second, how can we explain the picture of the basin as a daily renewal? Following Jesus may mean laying down one's life as it did for the ten twentieth century martyrs whose statues are on the west front of Westminster Abbey. Or it may mean a continuing commitment to Jesus in daily life. Elsewhere Jesus says to the disciples, *If any want to become my followers, let them deny themselves and take up their cross **daily** and follow me.(Luke 9:23)*

Third, how can we avoid the fate of Judas, the betrayer? William Temple offers the following stirring warning: 'We may go to Church and say our prayers and read our Bibles; the cleansing Word flows over us; but if our hearts are closed we are not cleansed.'

Prayer

Our Creating and Redeeming God, we thank you that Jesus calls us servants, messengers, disciples, and even friends. Help us to serve faithfully, to speak truly, to learn consistently and to live lovingly. Lord, we are glad that you honour our beginnings as believers. Strengthen and guide us to meet the demands of going on to maturity as we look to Jesus the pioneer and perfecter of our faith. Amen.

Discussion

1. How does the parable of the bathtub and the basin deepen our perceptions about the life of God's new age?
2. Why did Jesus originally tell the parable of the bathtub and the basin?
3. What is a contemporary meaning of the parable of the bathtub and the basin for us?

11   THE FATHER'S HOUSE

In my Father's house there are many dwelling places. If it were not so, would I have told you that I go to prepare a place for you? And if I go and prepare a place for you, I will come again and will take you to myself, so that where I am, there you may be also.
John 14:2-3

Category: What type of parable is it?

The parable of the Father's house is a parable of enduring love in the life of God's new age. Placement is a symbol for the relationship between Jesus and his disciples. As we shall see, Jesus uses the words *In my Father's house* near the Temple which he had called *my Father's house* and in the upper room where Jesus had his Last Supper with the disciples. Jesus is hinting that he brings a New Temple. He is also suggesting that the meeting in the upper room is a foretaste of God's eternal home. As a parable of enduring love in the life of God's new age, the Father's house assures the disciples of peace in their present and future experiences of grace and truth which come through Jesus Christ.

Context: When and where is the parable's situation?

The statement about *my Father's house* comes after an interchange between Peter and Jesus. Peter had asked, *Lord, where are you going?(John 13:36)* Jesus replied that Peter could not follow him now but he would do so later. Peter asked why not now because he was willing to lay down his life for Jesus. Then Jesus predicted Peter's denial. In this context Jesus gives promises to all his disciples, including Peter. Jesus is preparing them for the trial of his death and the triumph of his resurrection.

Content: How is the parable to be understood?

Jesus uses the words *In my Father's house* in twin circumstances. The group is near the Temple which Jesus had called *my Father's house (John 2:16)*. The group is also meeting for the Last Supper in *a large room upstairs* which Jesus calls *my guest room (Mark 14:14-15)*.

When Jesus gathers with his disciples they are worshippers in the New Temple. There people worship God in spirit and in truth. In spirit God's kind of life is enjoyed by believers. In truth, that is in Jesus, is the single basis of God's kind of life. As Jesus had said, *The hour is coming, and is now here, when the true worshippers will worship the Father in spirit and truth.(John 4:23)*

Jesus also turns the meeting in the upper room into a parable of eternity. The upper room foreshadows the heavenly home of God. Jesus says to the disciples, *I go to prepare a place for you ... I will come again and will take you to myself, so that where I am, there you may be also.*

The Gospels of Matthew, Mark and Luke along with Paul's first letter to Corinth tell of Jesus' Last Supper. An important element of that meal the night before Jesus died related to the future. Christians remembered Jesus in bread and wine and they were told by Paul, *as often as you eat this bread and drink the cup, you proclaim the Lord's death until he comes.(1 Corinthians 11:26)*

Jesus talks about *many dwelling places*. To say *many* is to say that there are enough for all. The word translated *dwelling places* has two associations. In the present Jesus can be referring to wayside shelters at stages along the road of life. Jesus goes ahead of his people and makes arrangements for resting places. This interpretation implies that if we are travelling in a heavenly direction, we are already in the Father's heavenly home.

By speaking of the future Jesus can be seen as referring to a permanent abiding place, in the sense of abiding with God. This understanding means that communion with God is a permanent and universal possibility. One is reminded of the vision of another John, the seer of Patmos, with his vision of a new heaven and a new earth in which *the home of God is among mortals.(Revelation 21:2)*

Jesus is preparing *dwelling places* by preparing people who are to dwell in them. We have the blessed assurance that Jesus has already brought heaven to earth for us. We also have the blessed hope that he will make all things new. Meanwhile, Jesus promises that *the Advocate, the Holy Spirit, whom the Father will send in my name, will teach you everything, and remind you of all that I have said to you. Peace I leave with you; my peace I give to you ... Do not let your hearts be troubled, and do not let them be afraid.(John 14:26-27)*

In summary, Jesus uses the words *In my Father's house* near the Temple which he had called *my Father's house* and in the upper room where he had his Last Supper. Jesus talks about *many dwelling places* including a present association of wayside shelters at stages along the road of life and a future association of a permanent abiding place. Meanwhile, Jesus promises believers the Holy Spirit and his peace.

Connection: Why does the parable apply now as it did then?

Life in society stands and falls by the way family units are functional or dysfunctional. A house is not necessarily a home, but it should be. If members of a household care for each other and treat each other with respect, life at home can build up and not tear down. Life in God's society operates the same way. Church groups are meant to be safe and peaceful places where people learn to trust each other as people who share the present and future in the company of the Lord of the Church.

The parable of the Father's house has interesting associations for modern families and churches.

First, why are followers of Jesus troubled and distressed? A football coach announced his resignation. He gave two reasons: illness and fatigue. The fans had become sick and tired of him! Yet the stresses of life confront us all: change, family life, work loads, injury or sickness. If we are seekers after mature faith life provides plenty of experiences for putting faith into practice.

Second, how can we, like the disciples, experience the many dwelling places in the Father's house? The supports of Christian faith can be experienced in the regular patterns of home, work, sports, hobbies, worship, and study. These supports can also be available in the crises of life such as during pregnancy and birth, childhood and adolescence, courtship and marriage, employment and unemployment, old age and death.

Third, how does Jesus give peace of mind? In classical Greek peace meant the cessation of war or strife. In the Old Testament it related to the restoration of harmony between God and humankind. In the New Testament it included objectively the peace with God - the forgiveness of the truly sorry sinner reconciled to God through Christ - and subjectively the peace of God - the tranquillity of heart and mind resulting from the Holy Spirit's assurance of reconciliation with God.

Prayer

Our Creating and Redeeming God, we too seek to worship you in spirit and in truth. For now we need peace and refreshment along our path through life. In the future we look forward to the permanent abiding place of your eternal home. Thank you for the assurance of the Spirit of truth that as we travel heavenwards we are already in heaven, thanks to Jesus our Lord. Amen.

Discussion

1. How does the parable of the Father's house broaden our knowledge of the life of God's new age?
2. Why did Jesus originally tell the parable of the Father's house?
3. What does the parable of the Father's house say to us in our world?

12   THE TRUE VINE

I am the true vine, and my Father is the vinegrower. He removes every branch in me that bears no fruit. Every branch that bears fruit he prunes to make it bear more fruit.
John 15:1-2

Category: What type of parable is it?

The parable of the true vine is a second Johannine parable about sharers in the life of the age to come. Jesus contrasts branches which bear no fruit with branches which bear fruit. Jesus himself is the true vine and his disciples are branches which bear fruit. By abiding in Jesus and his words and God's love they bear much fruit and experience much joy. The disciples participate in the life of the new age that comes in Jesus.

Context: When and where is the parable's situation?

Jesus is preparing his disciples in John 13-17 for his coming departure. They will have to face life after his death (John 18-19) and resurrection (John 20-21). The statement of Jesus about *the true vine* is in the context of two commands: *Abide in me* (John 15:1-8) and *Abide in my love* (John 15:9-17). Overall the passage makes the point that abiding in Christ and his love results in bearing fruit. The vine is the symbol of the people of God. Unlike the ancient people of God who failed to be fruitful, the followers of Jesus, both Jews and Greeks, by abiding in him and abiding in his love are fruitful.

Content: How is the parable to be understood?

The vine is a symbol of the ancient people of God who had failed to be fruitful. For example, Isaiah of Jerusalem says, *For the vineyard of the LORD of hosts is the house of Israel, and the people of Judah are his pleasant planting; he expected justice, but saw bloodshed; righteousness, but heard a cry! (Isaiah 5:7)* According to Jesus, the ancient people of God still fails to be fruitful. For instance, in the parable of the wicked tenants he says, *What then will the owner of the vineyard do? He will come and destroy the tenants and give the vineyard to others.(Mark 12:9)*

In the time of Jesus there was a great golden vine carved over the gate of the Temple, but all the Temple was destroyed in AD 70. At the end of Jesus' life, there is the fruit of the vine on the table at the Last Supper, and on the third day this dead Christ becomes the living Lord. The failed vine of the ancient people of God gives way to the successful vine of the people of God, Jew and Gentile alike, who abide in Jesus.

Jesus is the whole vine, the fruitful vine, with his branches, Jews and Greeks, who abide in him. *I am the true vine, and my Father is the vine-grower.* Jesus promises to cut off dead branches and to cut clean living branches. Jesus promises much fruit. *He removes every branch in me that bears no fruit. Every branch that bears fruit he **prunes** to make it bear more fruit.* And he continues: *You have already been **cleansed** by the word that I have spoken to you.(John 15:3)* There is a play on words *prunes ... cleansed* which is captured by the marginal note of the NRSV: 'The same Greek root refers to pruning and cleansing.' (James Moffatt in 1935 had translated *prunes* as 'cleans' and *cleansed* as 'clean'.)

The disciples as the branches must abide by faith in Jesus the vine. Then they will bear much fruit. *Those who abide in me and I in them bear much fruit, because apart from me you can do nothing.* The disciples also abide in the words of Jesus and the love of God. Then they will experience much joy. *I have said these things to you so that my joy may be in you, and that your joy may be complete.(John 15:11)*

The word *abide* occurs often in John's Gospel. It can be translated 'remain' or 'stay' or 'dwell'. To abide in Jesus and his love is the believer's basic duty. It is the act that defines truly Christian life. In Christ alone can Christians live. In him alone there is truly fruitful service to God. In him alone there is answered prayer. In him alone there is loving obedience. Those who abide in him are his friends. If they belong to him they are united with his friends in his love.

In summary, the vine is a symbol of the ancient people of God. According to Jesus, the ancient people of God still fails to be fruitful. Jesus is the whole vine, the fruitful vine, with his branches, Jews and Greeks, who abide in him. Jesus promises to cut off dead branches and to cut clean living branches. Jesus promises much fruit. The disciples as the branches of the vine must abide in Jesus by faith. In doing so, they will bear much fruit. The disciples also abide in the words of Jesus and the love of God. Then they will experience much joy.

Connection: Why does the parable apply now as it did then?

When people who enjoy the fruit of the vine visit Adelaide, they tend to go north to the Barossa Valley or south to McLaren Vale. These areas are notable for their spacious vineyards and wineries. Indeed, in Adelaide the South Australian climate is most conducive to fruit growing and vegetable plots. Even an inept gardener can enjoy growing fruit trees in the back yard. Such a gardener can learn the right time to plant, to water, to fertilise, to gather the fruit, and to prune. Jesus, who was once confused with a gardener on a significant occasion, must have known a good deal about gardening.

For the discerning reader the parable of the true vine brings to mind at least three connections.

First, what associations do vines, vine-growers, and branches have? An ancient Jewish prayer gives thanks for wine: 'Blessed are You, Lord, our God, King of the Universe, who creates the fruit of the vine.' In addition, a second century Christian prayer gives thanks for the cup at the Lord's Supper: 'We thank you, our Father, for the holy vine of David, your child, which you have revealed through Jesus, your child. To you be glory for ever.'

Second, how do believers abide in Christ? Glenn Hinson has suggested that a contemplative lifestyle includes three turnings:[1]

---

[1] See E. Glenn Hinson, *A Serious Call to a Contemplative Lifestyle* (Smyth & Helwys, 1993), pp. 48-51.

Turn on to God's presence in nature and in our neighbour.
Turn in by meditating on the Bible to find the mind of Christ.
Turn over by surrendering our lives to God.

Third, what 'fruit' results from abiding in Christ? In AD 155 the Bishop of Smyrna, Polycarp, died as a martyr because he refused the command of the Roman governor to curse Christ and to pledge his allegiance to Caesar. The response of Polycarp was succinct, 'Eighty-six years I have served him, and he never did me any wrong. How can I blaspheme my King who saved me?' Polycarp exercised widespread influence during his lifetime. His very name is Greek for 'Much Fruit'.

Prayer

Our Creating and Redeeming God, we *turn on* to your presence in nature and neighbour, we *turn in* by meditating on your Bible and finding your Son, and we *turn over* our lives to you in sweet surrender. Lord, help us to abide in you so that we may bear the fruits of true service, answered prayer, and loving obedience. Lord, thank you for being our friend and for uniting us together in love. Amen.

Discussion

1. How does the parable of the true vine add to our understanding of the life of God's new age?
2. Why did Jesus originally tell the parable of the true vine?
3. What does the parable of the true vine say to us in our world?

13 THE WOMAN IN CHILDBIRTH

When a woman is in labour, she has pain, because her hour has come. But when her child is born, she no longer remembers the anguish because of the joy of having brought a human being into the world.
John 16:21

Category: What type of parable is it?

The parable of the woman in childbirth relates to the crisis of the life of God's new age. As Jesus initiates God's new age he is the agent who fulfills God's purpose. Accordingly people then and now face crucial decisions. Will they identify in the short term with Jesus who goes to the cross and leaves an empty tomb? Will they identify in the long term with the final victory of God at the second coming of Jesus?

Context: When and where is the parable's situation?

Jesus is preparing his disciples in John 13-17 for his coming departure. They will have to face life beyond his death (John 18-19) and resurrection (John 20-21). The parable of the woman in labour is in the context of helpful statements about the work of the Holy Spirit (John 16:4b-15) and the victory of Jesus (John 16:25-33). In John 16:16-24 Jesus promises sorrowful joy. The conquest of evil comes in the midst of conflict.

Content: How is the parable to be understood?

The parable of the woman in childbirth has the following format:

When A occurs (*a woman is in labour ... has pain, because her hour has come*),
then B occurs (*her child is born, she no longer remembers the anguish*),
because C has occurred (*the joy of having brought a human being into the world*).

The structure of John 16:21 resembles that of Luke 11:21-22, the parable of the strong man:
When A occurs (*a strong man, fully armed, guards his castle, his property is safe*),
then B occurs (*one stronger than he attacks him ... overpowers him ... divides his plunder*),
because C has occurred (*he takes away his armour in which he trusted*).
Both parables are the words of Jesus, the master wordsmith, whose utterances are unforgettable.

The parable of the woman in childbirth draws on human experience at the time of the birth of a child. People can identify with the thoughts and feelings of proud parents, especially those of the mother.

The parable also draws upon the Old Testament. Isaiah of Babylon spoke of the exiles returning to Jerusalem in terms of childbirth: *a woman with child ... when she is near her time (Isaiah 26:17)* and *as soon as Zion was in labour she delivered her children (Isaiah 66:8)*. Interestingly, both Isaianic passages give hints of joy: *Your dead shall live, their corpses shall rise. O dwellers in the dust, awake and sing for joy! (Isaiah 26:19)* and *You shall see, and your heart shall rejoice (Isaiah 66:14)*. After the parable of the woman in childbirth Jesus alludes to

Isaiah 66:14 when he says, *So you have pain now; but I will see you again, and your hearts will rejoice, and no one will take your joy from you. (John 16:22)* Of course, this makes sense in the light of Jesus' death and resurrection, as well as in the light of his second coming.

The figure of birth pangs is not only evident in Isaiah 26:17 and 66:8, but it is also utilised by Jesus: *This is but the beginning of the birth pangs ... in those days there will be suffering ... after that suffering ... they will see 'the Son of Man coming in clouds' with great power and glory. (Mark 13:8,19, 24, 26)* There was the expectation of trials and tribulations before the coming of the Day of the Lord in the Old Testament and of the Son of Man in the New Testament.

The parable of the woman in childbirth has an immediate and distant focus. On the one hand, it relates to the death and resurrection of Jesus. The *pain* and *anguish* of the crucifixion of Jesus give way to the *joy* of the resurrection of the Son of God. On the other hand, it refers to the final victory of God at the second coming of Jesus, the Son of God. The *pain* and *anguish* of the Messiah's people will give way to the *joy* of the Messiah's triumph.

Just as the woman suffers *pain* and *anguish* for the sake of *joy* at the safe arrival of her child, so Jesus and his followers suffer evil and death with the sure and certain hope of the victory of God in the immediate and distant future.

In summary, the format of the parable of the woman in childbirth is as follows: When A occurs, then B occurs, because C has occurred. The parable draws on human experience at the time of the birth of a child. It also draws upon the Old Testament. The parable relates to the death and resurrection of Jesus and refers to the final victory of God at the second coming of Jesus.

Connection: Why does the parable apply now as it did then?

I remember very well the births of my son and daughter. When my son was born, I waited outside the delivery room until I was summoned to see my wife and our handsome baby boy. However, when my daughter was born, I was allowed to be present, to hold my wife's hand, to encourage her as she gave birth to our beautiful baby daughter. At first hand I learned that a mother forgets the pain of childbirth as she rejoices in the safe arrival of a healthy child.

The parable of the woman in childbirth has three possible associations today. First, in every day life is there no gain without pain? Britain's wartime Prime Minister, Winston Churchill, could easily have given up during the Battle of Britain. Yet in the dark hours of May 1940 he issued the challenge to his suffering citizens, 'I have nothing to offer but blood, toil, tears and sweat.'

Second, how does a follower of Jesus see pain giving way to joy? Oscar Romero was a bishop who identified with the poor and the persecuted in El Salvador. He said, 'I must tell you as a Christian, I do not believe in death without resurrection. If I am killed, I shall arise in the Salvadoran people.' He was shot dead in a church service on March 24, 1980. His memory is cherished by his fellow Salvadorans.

Third, what do we think about the explanation of God's victory in Jesus in terms of D-Day? Oscar Cullmann suggested that the death and resurrection of Jesus is D-Day and it precedes V-Day, the final victory of God in the second coming of Jesus.[1] June 6, 1944 was D-Day, the date of the Normandy invasion by the Allies. It was a decisive event which assured that complete and final victory was drawing near. V-Day was a day nominated to celebrate victory. May 8, 1945, V-E Day (Victory in Europe), followed Germany's surrender.

Prayer

Our Creating and Redeeming God, we contemplate the big picture of your ways in the world. We praise you that the pain of your Son's crucifixion gave way to the joy of his resurrection. We trust you that the pain of Christ's people will give way to the joy of his triumph. Lord, help us to endure the lows of life so that we will enjoy the highs of life here and hereafter. Through Jesus our Saviour. Amen.

Discussion

1. How does the parable the woman in childbirth contribute to our insights into the life of God's new age?
2. Why did Jesus originally tell the parable of the woman in childbirth?
3. What is the relevance of the parable of the woman in childbirth today?

---

[1] See Oscar Cullmann, *Christ and Time* (SCM Press, 1962).

Conclusion

At the end of our study of the Synoptic and Johannine parables, it is worthwhile to summarise their characteristics as literature, in history, and as theology.

As literary constructions, the parables are figurative sayings, similitudes, and story-parables. The Synoptic Gospels include all three, but the Fourth Gospel only has the first two types. However, both Synoptic and Johannine parables are memorable literary masterpieces. They capture the attention of readers and hearers. No one can forget the twists and turns of the longer parables such as the unforgiving servant, the labourers in the vineyard, and the talents in Matthew, or the good Samaritan, the rich fool, and the prodigal son in Luke. Nor can anyone overlook the vividness of the shorter parables like the traveller in the dark, the grain of wheat, the Father's house, or the true vine in John. As literature, the parables of Jesus catch us, make us think, and drive us to take action.

Yet the parables are not just literary constructions. They belong to the ministry of Jesus and to the mission of the church. Every parable is told and retold in actual historical situations. Jesus and his followers face occasions of conflict. In such situations, the parables are weapons of warfare. They correct misunderstandings, reprove malicious gossip, and challenge vicious opponents. For example, in the Synoptic Gospels the parable of the sower encourages the downhearted in their ministry with success in the midst of failure and with witness in the midst of struggle in the church's mission. Furthermore, with the parable of the ripe fields as found in John's Gospel, Jesus seeks to teach the disciples that he is active in their work as his messengers. The parable of the ripe fields also shows that the promise of the messianic age is coming true; Jesus treats the future as already present. Jesus and the Samaritans as told in John 4 foreshadow the apostles and the Samaritans as recorded in Acts 8.

Moreover, the parables in the Synoptic Gospels carry a theological message about God's kingdom while in the Fourth Gospel it is a theological message about eternal life. Interestingly, in the Synoptic Gospels, the parables represent about a third of Jesus' recorded words. In Joachim Jeremias' view, these parables in Greek are as close as possible as one can get to the very voice of Jesus in Aramaic. Accordingly, parables such as the hidden treasure and the costly pearl put us in direct contact with Jesus' proclamation of God's kingdom. In John's Gospel, on the other hand, there are about a dozen short parables. Through John's unique understanding, these parables speak of Jesus' teaching in terms of eternal life. Thus the parable of the apprentice son tells of enduring love in the life of God's new age while the parable of the true vine talks about the participants in the life of the age that comes in Jesus. Both parables disclose the mind of Christ in regard to his person and work.

Such is the literary, historical, and theological nature and purpose of the parables of Jesus in the Gospels. As Jesus intended, they remain stimulating, energising and groundbreaking for the discerning reader.

Select Bibliography

Part A: Synoptic Parables (in order of publication)

C.H. Dodd, *The Parables of the Kingdom* (First published 1935; Revised edition Fontana Books, 1961) These lectures of a preeminent Welsh scholar at Yale University emphasised the setting in the life and ministry of Jesus. This book became the foundation for last century study of the parables.

Joachim Jeremias, *The Parables of Jesus* (First published in English 1954; Revised edition SCM Press, 1963) Originally written during the second world war, this book by a humble German scholar built on Dodd's work and analysed the setting of the parables in the life and mission of the church.

Helmut Thielicke, *The Waiting Father: Sermons on the Parables of Jesus* (James Clarke, 1960) Entitled 'God's Picturebook' in German, the English translation of this collection of sermons introduced a great theologian and gifted preacher to the English speaking world.

A.M. Hunter, *Interpreting the Parables* (First published 1960; Revised edition SCM Press, 1964) This canny Scottish New Testament scholar gave a synthesis of the contributions of Dodd and Jeremias. His book became a classic for busy ministers and interested lay people.

Kenneth E. Bailey, *Poet & Peasant and Through Peasant Eyes: A Literary-Culteral Approach to the Parables in Luke* (First published 1976 and 1980; Combined edition Wm. B. Eerdmans Publishing Co., 1983) Bailey provides a distinctive Middle

Eastern exegesis of the parables as recorded in Luke's Gospel. He spent forty years living and teaching in theological institutes in Cairo, Beirut, Jerusalem and Nicosia. Bailey revisited the parables, among other things, in *Jesus Through Middle Eastern Eyes: Cultural Studies in the Gospels* (IVP Academic, 2008).

Robert Farrar Capon, *Kingdom, Grace, Judgment: Paradox, Outrage, and Vindication in the Parables of Jesus* (Originally published in three volumes 1985 1988 1989; Combined edition Wm. B. Eerdmans Publishing Co., 2002) While Capon classified the parables intriguingly within the Gospel accounts of the ministry of Jesus, at the same time he applied the parables to our time. The result is a unique series of quirky reflections.

Craig Blomberg, *Interpreting the Parables* (First published 1990; Second edition Apollos, 2012) This conservative scholar swims against the tide of scholarly opinion by treating the parables as allegories. Instead of one point per parable, Blomberg finds a range of possibilities. He also draws extensively on the secondary literature.

Peter Rhea Jones, *Studying the Parables of Jesus* (Smyth & Helwys, 1999) After a helpful introduction to studying the parables, and before a practical application to preaching the parables, Jones attractively examines twelve parables exemplifying the four major categories. His book is written with literary flair.

Arland J. Hultgren, *The Parables of Jesus: A Commentary* (Wm. B. Eerdmans Publishing Co., 2000) Hultgren combines introduction, translation, exegesis and exposition in his comprehensive and accessible treatment of the parables in Matthew, Mark and Luke. He even deals with parables in the so called Gospel of Thomas. Hultgren's commentary is a gold mine for readers of the parables.

Klyne R. Snodgrass, *Stories with Intent : A Comprehensive Guide to the Parables of Jesus* (Wm. B. Eerdmans Publishing Co., 2008) The subtitle says it all. Snodgrass has produced an encyclopedic volume about the parables of Jesus. He raises issues and provides options. He has drawn together a wealth of information.

Amy-Jill Levine, *Short Stories by Jesus: The Enigmatic Parables of a Controversial Rabbi* (HarperOne, 2014) In utilising ancient Jewish rabbinical sources, Levine separates the parables from the one who told them and from the gospel writers who recorded them. When she transposes the parables into modern times, she removes any anti-Judaism bias. She gives a quite idiosyncratic layer of interpretation.

Part B: Johannine Parables (in order of English publication)

William Temple, *Readings in St. John's Gospel* (Macmillan,1952) Archbishop of Canterbury from 1942 until his untimely death in 1944, Temple left a profoundly moving series of devotional meditations on John's Gospel.

C.H. Dodd, *The Interpretation of the Fourth Gospel* (Cambridge, 1953) and *Historical Tradition in the Fourth Gospel* (Cambridge, 1963) This Welsh New Testament scholar's career concluded with these two major works on the Fourth Gospel, treating leading ideas, structure, narrative and sayings of Jesus.

Raymond E. Brown, *The Gospel according to John Vols. 1 & 2* (Doubleday, 1966, 1974) The American Roman Catholic's two encyclopedic volumes on John's Gospel present his translation with insightful introduction and comprehensive commentary.

A.M. Hunter, *According to John* (SCM Press, 1968) The helpful Scot produced a fine synthesis of Johannine studies as at 1968. His little masterpiece built on Dodd's identification of the parables of John's Gospel.

William E. Hull, 'John,' *The Broadman Bible Commentary*, 9:189-376 (Broadman Press, 1970) My doctoral supervisor contributed this brief, but brilliantly written, commentary to the Baptist commentary on the whole Bible in the 1970s. It is an ideal resource for teaching and preaching.

Rudolf Bultmann, *The Gospel of John* (Blackwell, 1971) The German Lutheran's interpretation of John's Gospel was controversial and comprehensive. His provocative understanding of the Gospel raised issues of method and content for fellow scholars.

William Barclay, *The Daily Study Bible: The Gospel of John Vols. 1 & 2* (Saint Andrew Press, 1975) The venerable Scot has left a worldwide fellowship of lay people and clergy who read for inspiration and enjoyment his translation and commentary on the entire New Testament.

C.K. Barrett, *The Gospel according to St. John Second Edition* (Westminster, 1978) The English Methodist scholar was a sound guide for the seeker after understanding of the major witnesses of the New Testament. His commentary on John is detailed and trustworthy.

R. Alan Culpepper, *Anatomy of the Fourth Gospel:A Study in Literary Design* (Fortress Press,1983) and *The Gospel and Letters of John* (Abingdon, 1998) Culpepper's *Anatomy* broke new ground in literary studies of the New Testament. His *Gospel and Letters* is very helpful for preaching and teaching. Culpepper is a fine guide for his readers.

David Wenham, *The Parables of Jesus* (IVP, 1989) Wenham deals mainly with the Synoptic parables in his clear and helpful book. However, he identifies and comments on two Johannine parables: the shepherd and the vine.

Gail R. O'Day, 'The Gospel of John,' *The New Interpreter's Bible*, 9:491-865 (Abingdon, 1995) American scholar O'Day is the author of the introduction, commentary and reflections alongside the New International Version and the New Revised Standard Version of the Fourth Gospel.

Ben Witherington III, *John's Wisdom* (John Knox, 1995) The American Methodist Witherington is a fine writer and an engaging speaker. His commentary combines treatment of the original setting of the text and the contemporary meaning for our world.

Eduard Schweizer, 'What about the Johannine Parables?' *Exploring the Gospel of John In Honor of D. Moody Smith*, pp.

208-219. Edited by R. Alan Culpepper and C. Clifton Black (Westminster John Knox Press, 1996) The Swiss New Testament scholar made some valuable observations about parables in John in the Festschrift for the American Moody Smith. Schweizer included the 'I am' sayings in the parables.

Tom Wright, *John for Everyone Parts 1 and 2* (SPCK, 2002) Formerly Bishop of Durham in the Church of England and now Research Professor at the University of St Andrews, Wright is the accomplished author of academic and popular treatments of the New Testament. *John for Everyone* is a valuable resource for educated lay people.

Andrew T. Lincoln, *The Gospel according to Saint John* (Hendrickson, 2005) Lincoln provides a worthy addition to the Black's New Testament series. In his introduction, translation and commentary, he pays particular attention to historical, literary and theological matters.

Doug Rowston, *Jesus and Life: Word Pictures in John's Gospel* (GRACE & PEACE BOOKS, 2021) After treating the 'I am' sayings, this small book included my first attempt at explaining the context, content and connections of the parables of eternal life.

www.ingramcontent.com/pod-product-compliance
Lightning Source LLC
Chambersburg PA
CBHW030256010526
44107CB00053B/1737